INSOMNIA

The Essential Guide

Need —2— Know

Antonia Chitty & Victoria Dawson

First published in Great Britain in 2009 by
Need2Know
Remus House
Coltsfoot Drive
Peterborough
PE2 9BF
Telephone 01733 898103
Fax 01733 313524
www.need2knowbooks.co.uk

Contents

Introduction

Up to two in five people will suffer from insomnia at some point in their lives. Lack of sleep can make you feel depressed, slow down your body's healing mechanism and increase older people's risk of falls. Elderly people and women are more likely to suffer from insomnia but men can also be affected.

Sleep can seem simple when you don't have problems with it, but once you start to experience difficulties it can be hard to deal with. There are many factors that contribute to a good night's sleep including:

- What you eat and drink.
- Your night time environment.
- Exercise.
- Medical conditions.
- Stress.
- Whether you have any psychological problems.

This book will show you how to determine the cause of your sleep problems, which may include more than one factor. The second half of the book is packed with ideas to help you improve your sleep.

The information in this book is suitable for anyone who has sleep problems, and for parents of teenagers with insomnia. If you have a baby or younger child with sleep problems, you need more specialist help. You should talk to your doctor or health visitor about support for dealing with sleep problems. In some areas there are specialist children's sleep support services; some are NHS funded, others are run by charities or are private businesses. Your health visitor may be able to find out what is available locally to you. If your child has a special need, you may wish to contact Sleep Solutions. Their details can be found at the end of this book.

How much sleep does an adult need?

Are you getting enough sleep each night? Some people can manage with less sleep than others, but the average adult starts noticing problems if they don't achieve around seven to nine hours of sleep every night.

About the stages of sleep

Humans have two different types of sleep:

- REM (rapid eye movement) sleep, when most memorable dreaming takes place. 20-25% of total sleep time for most adults occurs in four or five separate parts. Your body is very relaxed in this phase. You may enter a period of lighter sleep or wake after REM sleep.

- Non-REM sleep. 75-80% of total sleep time, mostly without dreams. You may move your arms and legs in this phase, which is also when sleepwalking occurs.

In a normal sleep cycle you will move between REM and non-REM sleep, with more REM sleep taking place as the night progresses.

Disclaimer

This book is for general information about insomnia only. Anyone with serious concerns about their health or insomnia should contact their doctor or healthcare professional. This book can be used alongside professional medical advice but is not intended to replace it.

Chapter One

What is Insomnia?

Signs that there may be a problem

If you have difficulty falling asleep, you may have insomnia. People who are able to fall asleep but then wake and cannot get back to sleep may also have this condition. Any sleep you do have may seem insufficient and you may not feel refreshed. For sleep problems to be categorised as insomnia, you need to have problems three or more times each week for at least a month. The final element of insomnia is that your lack of night time sleep gives you problems during the day. You may simply find that you are tired and yawn a lot, or it may be difficult to concentrate and remember things. Some people feel the need to sleep during the day, but this is not necessarily part of the condition. Ongoing insomnia may also make you feel depressed.

Why we need sleep

It is not entirely clear why we need sleep, but it's obvious that it is vital to our health and wellbeing. Other reasons include:

- During sleep your body restores and heals itself.

- There are increased levels of some hormones at night.

- Sleep seems to be particularly important for keeping your brain functioning well. Regular sleep helps with memory and problem solving and reduces your risk of accidents.

How much sleep do we need?

Most adults need around seven to nine hours of sleep to remain alert during the day, although this varies from person to person. Some research has shown that people who sleep for six to seven hours each night live longer than those who sleep for a greater time. However, you can't extend your life span by simply setting the alarm clock as this only applies to people who wake naturally after six to seven hours.

Sleep and your age

'Most adults need around seven to nine hours of sleep to remain alert during the day, although this varies from person to person.'

A new baby's sleep pattern is very different to that of an adult or older person.

When we are born we need up to 18 hours of sleep each day. Much of this is spent in REM sleep, which is thought to contribute to brain development. As REM sleep is often followed by a period of lighter sleep or waking, you can see why babies sleep for short periods then wake, whereas adults aim for a solid block of sleep.

The amount of sleep needed decreases as a child grows up. Three to five-year-olds need around 11-13 hours of sleep during the night as most children have given up napping during the day by then. By the age of five or so, only a little over two hours are spent in REM sleep. Pre-teens may need between nine and 11 hours of sleep, while teenagers need nine to 10 hours.

As we age, the need for sleep alters, and around half of older people complain of regular sleep problems. Older people may not need less sleep but may find themselves spending less of the night in deep sleep. Hormone levels change, often leaving older people struggling to get to sleep, waking early and then needing to nap during the day. Poor health or a less active lifestyle can also reduce the ability to sleep for a solid seven or eight hours.

Men, women and sleep

Women are more likely to experience insomnia than men. Insomnia affects between 15% and 30% of men, and 25% to 40% of women.

In a National Sleep Foundation study, almost two-thirds of women aged from 18 to 64 had between one and three disturbed nights every week, and almost 70% said they frequently experience a sleep problem. This compares to just 52% of men who say they suffer insomnia a few nights a week or more.

Changing hormone levels during the menstrual cycle can leave women finding it harder to sleep during menstruation. Childbearing leaves women with an acute sensitivity to the sounds her baby makes which persists even once the baby is sleeping through the night. Later on in life, the menopause (particularly night sweats and hot flushes) can make it hard for women to sleep.

Sleep apnoea, a pause in breathing during sleep, can be a problem for men and women. And snoring can affect either sex, whether you are the one snoring or the one listening!

When we fall asleep

The circadian clock is your inner timekeeper. It works with a body chemical, adenosine, which is created throughout the day and causes sleepiness as its levels build. Daylight also influences your body clock – as light dims, your body creates more melatonin, giving your body another signal that it is time to sleep. Melatonin is a hormone that is produced especially at night in the pineal gland. Its secretion is stimulated by darkness. Melatonin is produced to help our bodies to regulate our sleeping and waking cycles.

What happens if we don't get enough sleep?

Sleep helps your body work correctly. There are some things that happen to everyone if they experience a broken night. You may look pale, with dark circles under your eyes. Your memory concentration and reaction time will be worse than usual. Perhaps you will yawn and feel sleepy. Lack of sleep can also make you irritable or give you a headache. You may even have blurred vision or slurred speech.

'Women are more likely to experience insomnia than men. Insomnia affects between 15% and 30% of men, and 25% to 40% of women.'

If all this can happen after a single night of disturbed sleep, it is unsurprising that a bout of insomnia can have further consequences. You may feel physically exhausted, with aching muscles. Lack of sleep can also cause other physical symptoms. Your digestive system can be affected, leading to problems including:

- Nausea.

- Loss of appetite.

- Weight loss or weight gain.

- Constipation.

Insomnia has an effect on your immune system, meaning that you could get sick more often and wounds may take longer to heal. Symptoms can include:

- Dizziness.

- Fainting.

- Hand tremors.

- Raised blood pressure.

A long term lack of sleep can more than double the risk of death from cardiovascular disease. Short sleep has also been shown to be a risk factor for Type 2 diabetes.

Some serious problems can occur if you miss sleep over a longer period of time. You may experience psychiatric or neurological disorders such as:

- Depression (up to 90% of patients with depression have sleep difficulties).

- Alcoholism.

- Delirium.

- Depersonalisation (a feeling of detachment).

- Hyperactivity.

- Psychosis-like symptoms (hallucinations, delusions, disorganised thinking).

- Bipolar disorder (abnormally elevated moods followed by depression).

'A long term lack of sleep can more than double the risk of death from cardiovascular disease. Short sleep has also been shown to be a risk factor for Type 2 diabetes.'

Types of insomnia

Transient insomnia

If you have insomnia for a few days or weeks, it is known as transient insomnia. This can be down to a number of causes:

- Change in your environment, such as being away from home.
- Environmental disturbances (noise, light, heat or cold).
- Stress (due to an upcoming event, perhaps).
- Physical illness or discomfort.
- Certain medications.

It can result in many of the symptoms that have already been discussed. Sometimes it is easy to spot the cause; you may realise that your normal sleep patterns will return once a period of stress or illness is over, making transient insomnia easier to deal with.

Acute insomnia

If you have disturbed sleep for any period from three weeks to six months, you may be suffering from acute insomnia.

This can be caused by:

- Physical illness or discomfort.
- Certain medications.
- Emotional distress.
- Stress (from exams, job loss or change, death, divorce, moving).
- Environmental disturbances (noise, light, heat or cold).
- Disturbed sleep patterns (jet lag, shift work).

Chronic insomnia

Men and women with chronic insomnia experience poor sleep for more than a year. Often there is no obvious cause. Chronic insomnia has a range of effects including:

- Physical and mental fatigue.
- Double vision.
- Hallucinations.

Patterns of insomnia

Onset insomnia

Onset insomnia simply means you have difficulty falling asleep. People with onset insomnia take more than 30 minutes to fall asleep. It may be linked with anxiety problems. Running through the day's events repeatedly or stressing about the day to come can stop you from winding down.

Middle insomnia

Middle insomnia or sleep maintenance insomnia occurs if you can drop off to sleep with relative ease but wake in the middle of the night and can't get back to sleep. It can take more than 30 minutes for someone with middle insomnia to fall asleep again.

Terminal insomnia

This means that you wake too early, after less than six and a half hours of sleep. You may feel that you need more sleep to get through the day but can't get back to sleep. Terminal insomnia can be linked to clinical depression.

What causes insomnia?

There are a number of factors which determine whether you are likely to get insomnia:

- Predisposing factors: these factors are the personal characteristics that make some people more likely to have disturbed sleep. Are you naturally anxious or prone to worry?

- Precipitating factors: have you had disruption in your life recently? This could be anything; the birth of a child, a break up or a loss.

- Perpetuating factors: these are the factors that prevent you getting over insomnia. For example, spending too long in bed, daytime napping or simply beginning to associate your bedroom with a frustrating lack of sleep.

Other sleep disorders

There are plenty of other conditions that can cause broken sleep. Read through this list to see if any might apply to you; it is important to understand what is causing your sleeplessness before looking to treat it.

Always talk to your doctor to get medical advice before starting a course of action. They will be able to advise whether other medical conditions might be involved with your sleep problems. You can also talk to your doctor or pharmacist to see if any existing prescription medication you are taking might be causing your sleep problems.

Bruxism

Some people experience disturbed sleep because they grind their teeth in the night. This is known as Bruxism. You might be unaware of it, but your dentist may be able to see the signs of wear on your teeth. Alternatively, you can get headaches and jaw pain as a result of the grinding. However, Bruxism can be treated by wearing a professionally fitted mouth guard overnight. Botulinum toxin (Botox) has also been used to relax the muscle that causes the grinding.

Delayed sleep phase syndrome

If you fall asleep at the same time most days and wake after around eight hours but your sleep time does not fit in with society's norms, you may have delayed sleep phase syndrome (DSPS). This is also known as circadian rhythm sleep disorder or delayed sleep phase type. The condition affects about three adults in 2000 people, but it is more common in teenagers, where around seven in 100 could be affected.

Characteristically, people with DSPS are wide awake until the early hours of the morning, whether they lie down to sleep earlier or not. They then fall asleep and remain asleep until mid morning or afternoon. Occasionally, they may even skip an entire night of sleep then sleep for 12 to 18 hours.

People with DSPS do sleep well throughout the morning or afternoon, unlike insomniacs who still have difficulty sleeping regardless of time of day. They can also drop off easily but only at the right time for their body clock. They cannot reset their body clocks by simply rising earlier and going to bed earlier.

Treatments include light therapy, melatonin or resetting the time of sleep commencement. It may be difficult to totally set the body clock to 'normal' hours and treatment may need to be repeated as the problem often recurs.

Someone with DSPS may feel like they have permanent jet lag if they try to stick to the hours needed for a traditional 9 to 5 job. Others adapt their lifestyle to fit their body clock – choosing a job with hours to fit your sleep pattern may be a more long term solution.

Sleep apnoea

In this condition, breathing stops momentarily while you are asleep. You are unlikely to be aware of the disturbance in breathing but may feel fatigue the following day as the condition also disturbs your sleep.

A 'sleep study' over night in a lab may be needed to diagnose this condition. If diagnosed, it can be treated using a continuous positive airway pressure (CPAP) device to provide a constant flow of pressured air that holds your airway open during sleep. A mouthpiece is another option for mild sleep apnoea, and if these treatments don't help there are also surgical options available.

Narcolepsy

Narcolepsy is when you experience excessive daytime sleepiness. You may feel the need to fall asleep spontaneously during the day and be unable to keep yourself awake. Some people also experience sudden muscle weakness, known as cataplexy, which can mean they feel limp or drop to the floor. People with narcolepsy can also experience the following:

- Sleep paralysis: the inability to move or talk for a few seconds on waking.
- Hypnagogic hallucinations: vivid dreamlike experiences while dozing, falling asleep or awakening.
- Automatic behaviour: continuing to do things or talk while asleep. This behaviour is not remembered on waking.

Treatment can involve stimulant drugs and planning regular daytime naps of 10-15 minutes.

Parasomnias

Parasomnias include a range of disruptive sleep-related events:

- Sleep walking (could also include sleep-eating).
- Night terrors.
- Periodic limb movement disorder (sudden involuntary arm/leg movements).
- Acting out violent or dramatic dreams.
- Restless legs syndrome: compulsive need to move your legs.

'Sleep helps your body work correctly. Without one night of good sleep you can simply feel tired during the day. When you have a number of poor nights in a row, your body can experience a range of physical and mental effects.'

Quick action checklist

Start noting down your patterns of insomnia:

- Do you have occasional nights of sleeplessness?
- Do you have a few weeks of poor sleep?
- Is it a battle to sleep every night? If so, has it been this way for months or years?

Think about when you have problems sleeping:

- Do you have difficulty falling asleep?
- Do you wake in the middle of the night and find it hard to sleep again?
- Do you wake too early in the morning?
- Can you identify any possible stress in your life that may contribute to poor sleep?

Summing Up

Sleep helps your body work correctly. Without one night of good sleep you can simply feel tired during the day. When you have a number of poor nights in a row, your body can experience a range of physical and mental effects. There are different patterns of insomnia and many different causes. Identifying when you have trouble sleeping is the start of solving the problem.

'There are different patterns of insomnia and many different causes. Identifying when you have trouble sleeping is the start of solving the problem.'

Chapter Two

Physical and Physiological Causes of Insomnia

Before you can treat your insomnia, it can help if you get to the bottom of what is causing it. Sleepless nights may be due to a number of factors, e.g. if you're pregnant, you may find it hard to get comfortable and fall asleep. Eating chocolate and having a cup of tea before bed can raise your caffeine levels and make it harder to drop off. Medication and recreational drugs can also cause insomnia. Read this chapter to find out about possible causes and note which ones might apply to you. The next chapter looks at psychological causes of sleeplessness.

Fiona says: 'My insomnia is probably due to aches and pains from hip arthritis. It is also a bit of a habit. It became worse after the menopause – I wake up too hot even though I have a thin duvet and I go to bed cold.'

Caffeine

Due to their caffeine content, regular consumption of tea, coffee and cola drinks is one of the commonest causes of insomnia. Caffeine is a stimulant, and most people realise that a coffee before bedtime can keep them awake. However, you may not know that caffeine is also contained in tea and chocolate. The exact amount will depend on how strong you make your drink or how much chocolate you eat. If you regularly order large sized drinks or ask for an extra shot to be added to your coffee in a café, you could be doubling your caffeine intake.

'Due to their caffeine content, regular consumption of tea, coffee and cola drinks is one of the commonest causes of insomnia.'

Coffee	-	instant	60-100 mg/cup
Coffee	-	ground	80-135 mg/cup
Tea	-	40-75 mg/cup	
Cocoa	-	10-17 mg/cup	
Chocolate	-	60-70 mg/bar	
Cola	-	34-65 mg/can	
Energy drink	-	70-80mg/can (a few energy drinks can go as high as 280mg/can)	
Caffeine tablets	-	100-400mg per tablet	

NB: This is only an approximate guide as cup sizes vary.

Some medications also contain caffeine. If you have started taking a cold and flu remedy or other painkiller and find you can't sleep, read the label or ask the pharmacist.

To avoid sleep problems from caffeine, stick to around two caffeinated drinks each day, aiming to consume them in the morning if possible. Definitely avoid anything with caffeine in it during the evening. Stick to herbal teas, fruit juices or water, or go for a decaffeinated option if you really can't go without!

Other dietary causes of insomnia

Alcohol

Alcohol can make it seem easier to drop off, but you are more likely to have poor quality sleep, vivid dreams and wake needing to urinate in the night.

Sugar

Sugary snacks before bedtime can make it hard to sleep. If you do drop off, you may wake in the night when your blood sugar drops again.

Dairy

Some studies have linked dairy intolerance to insomnia. Dairy products may include food such as milk, yoghurt, cheese or fromage frais. In certain individuals, dairy products can cause excess mucus production which may contribute to snoring. On the other hand, dairy foods are a good source of L-tryptophan which contributes to the creation of melatonin. This is the basis of the idea to have a milky drink before bedtime.

More research is needed in this area, so seek medical advice before cutting out any food group.

Magnesium

Low magnesium levels may contribute to insomnia, but this has not yet been proven. A small study found magnesium to help in treating restless legs syndrome, another cause of insomnia. Foods rich in magnesium include rye, wild rice, green leafy vegetables, nuts, seeds, pulses, beans, bananas, avocados, garlic, prunes and dates.

Physical causes of insomnia

Health problems

If you are physically uncomfortable, it can be hard to sleep. Pain, hot flushes or itching can all contribute to a disturbed night. If you have a short term condition that you know will pass, it is easy to take a few days off to catch up with sleep, resuming your proper sleep pattern when your illness has passed. However, if you have a chronic pain problem, ongoing itching due to a condition like eczema or are going through the menopause, you may find you are experiencing insomnia over months or years. Read on to find out more about these and other medical conditions that cause insomnia.

'If you are physically uncomfortable, it can be hard to sleep. Pain, hot flushes or itching can all contribute to a disturbed night.'

Hyperthyroidism

The excess thyroid hormone produced in hyperthyroidism makes your body speed up many vital functions. It can make you feel restless during the day as well as finding it hard to sleep at night. Your doctor can check your thyroid levels and discuss treatment options to reduce the level of thyroid in your body.

Michaela says: 'I developed insomnia as part of an underlying auto-immune thyroid disorder, Graves' disease.'

Menstruation, pregnancy and the menopause

Women's hormones, particularly oestrogen, have a role to play in insomnia. Many women suffer from poor sleep the night before their period starts as their oestrogen level reaches a monthly low.

'Many women suffer from poor sleep the night before their period starts as their oestrogen level reaches a monthly low.'

In pregnancy both oestrogen and progesterone levels rise. This means you spend a greater part of each night in REM (dreaming) sleep because of the effect of these hormones. Have you ever noticed more disturbed sleep at certain times of the month? This is caused by the same hormones. Pregnancy aches and pains, such as backache, restless legs and heartburn, also contribute to light or broken sleep. If you are pregnant, take simple measures like cutting down on caffeine, taking gentle exercise during the day and having a warm bath before bedtime.

In the run up to the menopause, oestrogen levels drop. This can cause insomnia by itself as the associated hot flushes often cause women to wake. If this is affecting you, discuss the pros and cons of natural and drug treatments for the menopause with your doctor.

Neurological disorders

There are a range of conditions affecting the brain which can cause insomnia. These include:

- Parkinson's disease.
- Alzheimer's disease.

- Dementia.
- A history of traumatic brain injury.

The primary disease should be treated by a doctor, who will be able to look into how your condition affects your sleep patterns.

Pain

Chronic pain is often linked to insomnia, particularly back pain. Some people find that while trying to fall asleep, their pain becomes far more prominent and harder to ignore. Others can fall asleep when their painkillers are working but wake in the night as they wear off. Pain can also make it harder to achieve deep unbroken sleep.

If pain is causing your sleeplessness, start by talking to your doctor or physiotherapist about measures to address the root cause. Then discuss medication to improve pain control overnight. After that, you could look at other ways to improve your sleep as suggested in the following chapters, but always make sure you address the cause of the pain first.

Pruritus

Pruritus, better known as itching, can cause sleeplessness. Some skin diseases like dry skin and eczema are chronic conditions and can cause ongoing problems. For other people, the cause of itching can be hard to pin down. Talk to your doctor about finding the cause for the itching and discuss how that can be treated.

Restless legs syndrome

This is a compulsive need to move your legs. You may feel a burning, tickling or itching in the legs which is more noticeable at night when sitting or lying still. Talk to your doctor to explore what could be causing your restless legs. There are a range of conditions from iron deficiency to vein problems that can be identified as the underlying difficulty. Your doctor can suggest the most appropriate treatment which will also contribute to reducing your insomnia.

Jenny says: 'I developed insomnia after I was diagnosed with post viral fatigue syndrome which impacted on my sleep pattern.'

Medication, herbal remedies and drugs

There are many drugs that can adversely affect your sleep.

Over-the-counter remedies

Earlier in this chapter it was highlighted that painkillers and cold and flu remedies can include caffeine. Ephedrine or pseudoephedrine in decongestants is a stimulant which can cause disturbed sleep in some people.

If you suffer from tiredness during the day and use tablets like ProPlus, it is worth noting that each tablet contains the same amount of caffeine as a cup of coffee. These kind of tablets should be avoided if you are having sleep problems.

Prescription medication

There are many other prescription drugs that stimulate the nervous system and can make it hard for you to sleep. If you suspect this applies to you, do not stop taking prescription medicine without advice. Instead, talk to your doctor or pharmacist. You may simply need to alter the time of day that you take your medication in order to regain a good night's sleep.

Long term use or abuse of over-the-counter or prescription sleep aids can produce rebound insomnia.

Nicotine

Nicotine is a stimulant and can keep you awake. If you can't quit, avoid smoking within three hours of bedtime.

Herbal remedies

Some herbal remedies can also act as stimulants and affect sleep. As an example, guarana is a caffeine containing stimulant that is added to some food and drink products found in health food stores. Medical herbalist Dr Anne Walker says: 'The main thing to avoid too much of is caffeine. Other stimulatory herbs such as Siberian ginseng can cause problems if taken at night, but they are generally okay if taken in the day.'

Weight loss products

Some weight loss products contain ephedrine or pseudoephedrine, and may also contain caffeine. Be careful when purchasing any such products; the Internet has made it very easy to buy products which are banned in some countries, unregulated in others and have little or no safety record.

Illegal drugs

Illegal drugs including cocaine, amphetamines and MDMA can make you feel wired and unable to sleep. If drug use is a problem for you, seek help from a drug counselling service.

Lifestyle issues related to insomnia

There are a number of lifestyle related factors that can cause short or long term insomnia. Read on to find out more about these factors and to see if any of them might affect you.

Irregular sleep schedule

Any sort of irregular sleep schedule can cause difficulties in dropping off or staying asleep or can cause you to wake early:

- Shift work

If you work shifts, you are forcing yourself to follow a pattern of waking and sleeping that does not tie in with your body's natural circadian rhythm. Some shift workers can find it very hard to get good quality sleep if they need to sleep during daylight hours. A constantly changing pattern of shifts can make it even harder to sort out a sleep pattern.

- Jet lag

Like with shift work, jet lag means that the times your body needs to sleep are out of sync with the times allocated for sleep.

- Going to bed early

If you are tired from poor sleep, the temptation may be to go to bed early. However, this can lead to problems in itself. For example, if your body only needs seven hours of sleep and you go to bed at nine, you may be setting yourself up to wake in the early hours of the morning, experiencing broken sleep from 4am onwards and leaving you tired for the next day.

- Napping

Another way of dealing with a poor night's sleep is to have a nap the next day. However, a long nap can simply mean you have more sleep problems the next night. You may not be able to drop off when you want or wake in the middle of the night. If you need to nap, keep it to 15 to 30 minutes. Avoid naps close to bedtime as they can interfere with night time sleep.

Lack of exercise or activity

Sometimes it can be hard to sleep simply because you have not done enough during the day. If you have an inactive lifestyle, aim to slot in a little extra exercise every day. It does not have to be complex or expensive. For example, you could get off one bus stop early to give you a slightly longer walk each day. Lack of activity can be a particular problem for older people or those with physical limitations. If this is an issue for you, ask your doctor if there are programmes in your area to help you get active.

'If you have an inactive lifestyle, aim to slot in a little extra exercise every day. It does not have to be complex or expensive. For example, you could get off one bus stop early to give you a slightly longer walk each day.'

Age

Many people experience sleep problems as they get older. This is due to a change in the balance between REM and non-REM sleep. Older people have more periods of shallow or dreaming sleep and shorter periods of deep sleep. This can reduce your ability to sleep through the night.

Too much stimulation before bed

If you are working right up until 11 at night, it can be hard to switch off immediately. The same goes for playing exciting computer games or watching action movies. Even having a TV in the bedroom can make it a place of activity rather than rest. Try to come up with a routine to help you wind down before bed and opt for calming activities. See chapter 5 for more ideas.

Excessive noise or light

There are many factors that can disturb your sleep. If a noisy environment is the problem or your partner snores, try ear plugs, a white-noise machine (see chapter 5 for more information) or separate bedrooms. If light is a problem, look at whether blackout blinds will help.

See chapter 5 for more information on creating a peaceful sleeping environment.

Lack of sunlight

The rhythms that help your body know when to sleep and when to wake are partly dependent on your exposure to daylight. Bright sunlight tells your body it is daytime which improves your sleep-wake cycles. Most artificial indoor lighting does not have the same effect.

Try to get at least two hours of sunlight a day. If you have problems achieving this, you may want to look into using a light box. This is simply an enclosed box containing fluorescent tubes, fitted with a screen to diffuse the light. The treatment involves sitting in front of the lamp for a set period of time each day. A range of suppliers can be found on the Internet.

Who can help?

If you suspect any of the issues in this chapter are contributing to your sleepless nights, start by talking to your doctor. It is important to get to the bottom of the cause of your insomnia before taking steps to deal with it.

A pharmacist is available to consult at your local pharmacy. If you take in details of any medication you are on, they will be able to check if these could be contributing to your insomnia. Always get professional advice before cutting down or stopping medication.

Quick action checklist

- Spend some time looking at your sleep habits.
- Consider which factors could be contributing to your sleep problems.
- Consider consulting a doctor at this stage to get to the bottom of the cause of your insomnia.

Summing Up

There are many different causes of insomnia. Take the time to think about what could be causing your problems. This is a good time to talk to a medical professional if you are at all unsure about the cause or if you suspect a health problem, medication or addiction may be the root of your sleeplessness.

Chapter Three

Psychological Causes of Insomnia

Very often, insomnia is due to some sort of stress in your life. You may have experienced a sleepless night before an event like an exam, but what happens with long term stress? Life problems like bereavement, fear, stress, anxiety, emotional or mental tension, work issues or financial stress all contribute to insomnia. It can be a vicious circle as insomnia can cause problems too. One survey found that people with insomnia were more likely to feel depressed, lack concentration and have memory problems.

Finding and addressing the underlying cause of insomnia is usually necessary to cure it, so this chapter looks at the psychological causes of insomnia.

Stress

Stress is a big factor in sleep disturbance. Have you ever laid awake, running through your worries in your head? Perhaps you have woken in the night and started thinking about the next day's problems? It's easy to get into a pattern where it is impossible to switch off negative thoughts and relax into sleep.

Short term stress

You may be aware of a stressful event coming up that is disrupting your sleep. If you have a job interview, you may sleep badly the night before. Teenagers in the middle of exams often suffer from stress – see chapter 10. You may have had a row with someone and are unable to stop thinking about it.

'Life problems like bereavement, fear, stress, anxiety, emotional or mental tension, work issues or financial stress all contribute to insomnia.'

Medium term stress

Major life events can cause stress. If you take a step back you may be able to identify when you are finding it hard to drop off. Even if the life event is positive, like a forthcoming wedding, you may find yourself running through lists of things to do when you would rather be sleeping. Other major life events like birth, divorce and bereavement can also lead to insomnia.

- Birth: many new parents find the first few months after birth stressful. You are suddenly responsible for a tiny vulnerable human being, and it can be hard to switch off from this responsibility. Despite sleepless and broken nights, you may find yourself lying awake listening to see if your baby is still sleeping safely. Some parents with children who regularly wake in the night over a long period can just get out of the habit of a solid night of sleep.

- Divorce: a divorce, much like bereavement, can turn every aspect of your life upside down, so it is unsurprising that it can cause stress leading to insomnia. Because divorces can be long and drawn out, it is easy to see that insomnia can become a chronic problem for some people.

- Bereavement: insomnia can be common after the loss of a loved one. You may find it hard to sleep in the short term, but bereavement can cause insomnia which lasts for months or more. If you have not gone through a grieving process, stress and insomnia can recur years or decades after the death.

'If you have problems sleeping, this can become a source of stress in itself. You can become tense in the run up to bedtime, anticipating another broken night.'

John says: 'When I was going through my divorce, my sleep became disrupted. When I got into bed at night, I was truly exhausted. The problem was that I started to think about the divorce. Where would I live? Would I get custody of our child? I'd try hard to shut out the thoughts and then I'd start to clock watch and tell myself that I must go to sleep otherwise I wouldn't be able to function the next day and deal with all these issues. It was a vicious circle. Counselling really helped. I was able to share my worries and start to identify positive ways to deal with them.'

Sleep related stress

If you have problems sleeping, this can become a source of stress in itself. You can become tense in the run up to bedtime, anticipating another broken night.

Nell says: 'I used to lie awake worrying that I wasn't sleeping.'

Stress and your health

Any sort of mental stress is harder to cope with if you are physically run down. Look at improving your physical health and lifestyle to help manage a difficult period. Make sure you are eating well and limiting caffeine, nicotine and alcohol – all of which can contribute to insomnia. Have a regular bedtime routine and learn some relaxation techniques to help switch off mentally.

Mary explains: 'It started when I was about 16, around the same time I started work. I guess the fact that I knew I had to be up early the next day meant that I became a bit paranoid about getting enough sleep.'

Depression

Depression can cause insomnia. Characteristically, people who are depressed can fall asleep but wake in the early hours and find it hard to get back to sleep. However, insomnia over a period of time can also lead to depression or be an indicator that depression is on its way. The way you sleep changes when you're depressed, with a more rapid descent into REM (dreaming sleep) which lasts for longer periods. This change in the composition of sleep can affect memory and learning.

Veronique's experience of insomnia started with depression: 'I had a bout of depression after my third child, caused by overdoing it. My children are six, five and three, so when my last little boy was born the others were still quite demanding. I also run my own business and co-run two others. My partner has a farm that I occasionally help out on. I guess I just got too tired and then the depression started, along with panic attacks and claustrophobia and, of course, the lack of sleep and being unable to sleep. This was made worse by my fear of not waking up when I did fall asleep.'

Anxiety

Anxiety can be a normal response to stress or danger. However, it can become hard to stop being anxious and wind down for bed. You may have physical symptoms like a rapid heartbeat, headache, stomach ache or breathlessness. It is difficult to sleep when you are in this condition.

'Depression can cause insomnia. Characteristically, people who are depressed can fall asleep but wake in the early hours and find it hard to get back to sleep.'

If you can't stop feeling anxious, you may have an anxiety disorder. Persistent and ongoing anxiety can be triggered by a stressful life event. The condition can also be related to misuse of alcohol or long term use of benzodiazepines as they can cause insomnia. It may take some time to resolve this sort of insomnia as stopping benzodiazepines can cause sleep problems.

Treatment may involve psychotherapy alongside prescription of anxiolytics or antidepressants to deal with symptoms.

Other psychiatric disorders

Dementia

Dementia, or Alzheimer's disease, is a condition where mental abilities like thinking, remembering and reasoning decrease, usually over a period of time. It is most common in those over 85 but can occur even in the under 65s. Sleep can become disturbed as you become confused and less aware of the cycle of day and night. You may have difficulty falling asleep or staying asleep, making your other problems worse.

Treatment of Alzheimer's disease is currently limited to aiming to slow the progress of the disease and deal with accompanying symptoms like depression. One research study (see below) shows that people with Alzheimer's can still benefit from advice to help with insomnia, such as getting exercise during the day and having a regular bedtime routine. For more information, see *Alzheimer's - The Essential Guide* (Need2Know).

Current treatments for sleep disturbances in individuals with dementia (Deschenes CL, McCurry SM)

Sleep disturbances are widespread among older adults. Degenerative neurologic disorders that cause dementia, such as Alzheimer's disease and Parkinson's disease, exacerbate age-related changes in sleep, as do many common comorbid medical and psychiatric conditions. Medications used to treat chronic illness and insomnia have many side effects that can further disrupt sleep and place patients at risk for injury. This article reviews the neurophysiology of sleep in normal aging and sleep changes associated with common dementia subtypes and comorbid conditions. Current pharmalogic and nonpharmalogic evidence-based treatment options are discussed, including the use of light therapy, increased physical and social activity, and multicomponent cognitive-behavioural interventions for improving sleep in institutionalised and community-dwelling adults with dementia.

Bipolar disorder

Bipolar disorder is characterised by periods of depression and periods of mania or high activity, short attention span and poor judgement. During these manic periods, which last for a week or more, you may feel little need for sleep. During depressed periods you might feel fatigued most of the time and have disturbed sleep. Treatment can involve medication and psychotherapy. Too little sleep can actually cause mania in someone prone to bipolar disorder, so it is important to maintain regular sleep habits.

Post traumatic stress disorder

This is an anxiety disorder resulting from exposure to a traumatic event. This can cause you to remain hyper-vigilant even after the danger has long passed, leading to difficulties relaxing and hence insomnia. Treatment mainly involves psychotherapy, but medication can also help with some symptoms.

Mina says: 'My insomnia was due to trauma and stress which started after I was woken by a burglar in my bedroom with a knife.'

Schizophrenia

This condition typically starts in young adulthood and causes delusions, hallucinations and disorganised thinking. Disorganised thinking and poor self care can wreck the sleep routine of a person with schizophrenia. The condition can also be accompanied by substance abuse which also affects sleep. Schizophrenia is treated with antipsychotic medication. Psychotherapy can also be used.

Obsessive compulsive disorder

In this condition, intrusive, repetitive thoughts can lead to compulsive behaviours. Consequently, you feel driven to do things repeatedly even though they may seem illogical. If you have OCD it can also be hard to switch off to sleep. OCD is treated using behavioural therapy and medication.

Medication for psychological problems

Sometimes the medication you are prescribed to help with a psychological problem can contribute to insomnia. If you are finding it hard to sleep, do not stop taking your medication. Stopping medication suddenly can cause serious problems. Instead, talk to your doctor. Ask if spreading the dose differently or taking the tablets at a different time of day might help. There may even be an alternative medication that would cause fewer sleep problems. Your doctor may also be able to prescribe something compatible with your regular medication to help you sleep. See chapter 8 for more information about medication and insomnia.

'Sometimes the medication you are prescribed to help with a psychological problem can contribute to insomnia.'

Who can help?

If you suspect any of these issues are contributing to your sleepless nights, start by talking to your doctor. For short term stress, the doctor may be able to refer you to a counsellor. If your stress is related to relationship problems, you may want to talk to a counsellor with specific training in this area from an organisation such as Relate. If you are bereaved, the charity Cruse has a helpline. Contact details for both organisations can be found at the back of this book.

If your insomnia has a psychological basis, your doctor can treat you for the underlying cause or refer you to a specialist for appropriate treatment.

Quick action checklist

■ Look at your life. Are there areas that are causing you stress or unhappiness?

■ If you have problems dropping off at night or wake in the night, do you lie awake and worry?

■ Consider consulting a doctor at this stage to get to the bottom of the cause of your insomnia.

Summing Up

Stress, anxiety, depression, psychological and mental health problems all have a strong link to poor sleep. Check out what could be causing your problem before moving on to use some of the tips in the following chapters.

Chapter Four

Diagnosing Insomnia

If you still have sleep problems and have taken simple measures like cutting out caffeine later in the day, you should talk to your doctor. Chapters 2 and 3 have looked at the wide range of problems that can cause insomnia. This chapter looks at what you can do yourself to find the cause of your sleep problems and how medical professionals can help too.

Keeping a sleep diary

A sleep diary helps to show when you went to sleep, how long for and whether you were disturbed in the night. You can also write in details of what you did during the day. This can shed light on whether sleep problems are only occurring during the working week, perhaps due to work related stress. You could also include details of what you eat and drink and any exercise that you do. Write down how you feel each day and when you start to feel tired.

How a sleep diary can help

- The act of filling in the diary every day can help you identify and deal with causes of insomnia.

- If you are going to talk to your doctor about sleep problems, a sleep diary can help them get to the bottom of your problem.

- A sleep diary can ensure that professionals take your problem seriously.

- If you start a new treatment or routine, the diary can show you and your doctor if it is working.

'A sleep diary helps to show when you went to sleep, how long for and whether you were disturbed in the night. You can also write in details of what you did during the day.'

Completing your sleep diary

- Keep the sleep diary by the side of your bed so that you can easily find it.

- Try to fill the diary in as soon as possible so that the information that you record is accurate.

- Be honest when completing the diary and make sure you record all the relevant information.

- Keep the diary for at least one week (preferably two) so that any patterns emerging can be identified.

On page 42 there is an example of a completed sleep diary to show you how one person has filled it in. Use the blank version on page 44 to make your own diary notes.

Sleep diary example

Jane has problems dropping off to sleep some nights and wakes for an hour or so in the small hours most mornings. Look at what she drinks during the day for a clue to why she can't switch off at night. However, this may not explain why she is waking at 3, 4 or 5am.

Jane should try cutting down on coffee and avoiding it completely in the late afternoon and evening. On some nights her alcohol consumption may be contributing to poor sleep. She could also avoid her habitual half bar of chocolate every evening as that also contains caffeine. If this does not stop her waking in the night, she should consult a doctor as early waking can be linked to depression.

Visiting your doctor

If simple remedies like cutting out caffeine and having a relaxing bedtime routine have not improved your sleep, you should see your doctor.

What your doctor will ask about

It really helps if you have kept a sleep diary as your doctor is likely to ask you about your lifestyle and sleep habits. Look at the list of questions below and think about your answers so you are prepared.

Questions your doctor might ask:

- When do you go to bed each night?
- When do you fall asleep?
- Do you wake during the night?
- When do you wake in the morning?
- How much alcohol do you drink each day?
- How much caffeine do you drink each day?
- Do you smoke? If so, how many each day?
- Do you take any drugs?

Your doctor may also ask about your general lifestyle habits, your diet and how much exercise you do.

The doctor should check your medical records for any history of illnesses which could cause sleep problems. They should also look at any medication you are taking to see if it can cause sleep problems

If you have kept a sleep diary, this will help the doctor get to the bottom of the cause of your insomnia. If not, your doctor may suggest you start keeping one.

'It really helps if you have kept a sleep diary as your doctor is likely to ask you about your lifestyle and sleep habits.'

Sleep patterns

Day / Date	1 August 7th	2 August 8th	3 August 9th	4 August 10th	5 August 11th	6 August 12th	7 August 13th
Did you nap?	No	No	Yes	Yes	No	No	No
Time and length of nap(s):			1.30pm, 15 mins	3pm 1.5 hours			
What time did you go to bed?	10pm	11.30pm	12.30am	9.30pm	10pm	10.15pm	10pm
When did you put your light out?	10.30pm	11.45pm	12.40am	9.45pm	11pm	10.45pm	10.15pm
Roughly when do you think you fell asleep?	11.30pm	12am	12.45am	11pm	12.15am	12.15am	12am
Did you wake in the night? What time(s) and for how long?	Yes, about 4am for an hour or so.	Yes, about 1.30am: toilet only, 3.30am: toilet only, 5.30am: toilet only.	Yes, about 2.30am: toilet only, 3.30am: toilet only, 5.30am - for an hour.	Yes, about 4.30am for an hour or so.	Yes, about 3am for an hour or so.	Yes, about 3.30am for an hour or so.	Yes, about 4.30am for 2 hours.
When did you finally wake in the morning?	7am	7.30am	8.30am	7am	7am	7am	7am
Total hours of sleep:	6.5	7ish	6.5ish	7	6ish	6ish	5
How would you rate your night's sleep: poor, average or good?	Average	Poor	Poor	Average	Average	Average	Poor

42

Food and drink - fill in the time and what you ate and drank. Note number of cups of tea, coffee, hot chocolate, cola, energy drinks, chocolate bars, etc.

Breakfast 7.45am	1 cup coffee	1 cup coffee	1 cup coffee	1 cup coffee	1 cup coffee	1 cup coffee	1 cup coffee
Morning	1 cup coffee, chocolate bar	1 cup coffee, chocolate bar	Croissant and another coffee		1 cup coffee, chocolate bar	1 cup coffee, chocolate bar	1 cup coffee, chocolate bar
Lunch 12.30ish	Sandwich, coke, apple, crisps	Sandwich, coke, apple, crisps		Brunch: eggs, fried bread, beans, sausage, bacon, tea	Sandwich, coke, orange	Sandwich, coke, banana, muffin	Sandwich, coke, Danish pastry
Afternoon	2x coffee, chocolate bar	2x coffee, chocolate bar	Omelette, chips, peas about 2.30pm		2x coffee, chocolate bar	2x coffee, chocolate bar	2x coffee, chocolate bar
Dinner Usually 7pm	Spaghetti bolognaise, cup of coffee		Sandwich	Chinese beef noodles	Salmon, salad, cup of coffee	Cheese on toast, cup of coffee	Chicken breast, potatoes, peas, cup of coffee
Evening	Chocolate – half a block	Curry at 9.30pm		Chocolate – half a block	Chocolate – half a block	Chocolate – half a block	Chocolate – half a block
Alcohol – type and number of drinks and time	1 glass red wine with dinner	3 bottles of lager	1 bottle of red wine		1 glass white wine with dinner		
What exercise did you do, when and how long for?	None	Gym, 12.30pm-1.30pm	None	None	None	Gym 12.30pm-1.30pm	None
Medication							
If you take medication, what medicines did you take and when?	None						
Medicines: Morning			Paracetamol				
Medicines: Afternoon				Proplus			
Medicines: Evening							

Day Date	1	2	3	4	5	6	7
Sleep patterns							
Did you nap?							
Time and length of nap(s):							
What time did you go to bed?							
When did you put your light out?							
Roughly when do you think you fell asleep?							
Did you wake in the night? What time(s) and for how long?							
When did you finally wake in the morning?							
Total hours of sleep:							
How would you rate your night's sleep: poor, average or good?							

Food and drink - fill in the time and what you ate and drank. Note number of cups of tea, coffee, hot chocolate, cola, energy drinks, chocolate bars, etc.

Breakfast							
Morning							
Lunch							
Afternoon							
Dinner							
Evening							
Alcohol – type and number of drinks and time							
What exercise did you do, when and how long for?							
Medication							
Medicines: Morning							
Medicines: Afternoon							
Medicines: Evening							

Getting a referral: what happens next?

Who you are referred to will depend on the cause of your insomnia.

If your doctor suspects that snoring is at the root of the problem, and you have tried simple solutions, you may need to see an ear nose and throat specialist who can deal with sinus problems.

You could be referred to see a clinical psychologist, particularly if the doctor thinks that your insomnia is due to a psychological cause like depression or anxiety. A psychologist can offer therapy such as Cognitive Behavioural Therapy (CBT) which has been shown to help with insomnia. Your doctor can refer you to local psychology services, but there may be a wait of several months for an appointment.

There might be a specialist NHS sleep clinic in your area. A sleep clinic can help with conditions including:

- Narcolepsy.
- Parasomnias.
- Periodic limb movements/restless legs syndrome.
- REM sleep behaviour disorder.
- Sleep apnoea.
- Snoring.

The clinic will have criteria as to who can be referred. You may be asked to complete an assessment test like the Epworth sleepiness scale to help the doctor assess whether the clinic will treat you. This asks you about how likely you are to doze off in various situations, such as when watching TV, as a car passenger or if you lie down for a rest. You respond with answers like: 'I would never doze in that situation' or 'I would have a high chance of dozing in such a situation'. Your responses are scored and can help to diagnose whether you have a condition such as obstructive sleep apnoea syndrome or narcolepsy. Some sleep clinics will only see patients with a score of 11 or more on this scale.

The clinic can offer specialist diagnostic techniques to work out the cause of your sleep problems and appropriate treatment. However, you may need to travel some distance to a sleep clinic if there is not one locally and there may be a long waiting time for an appointment.

The clinic will be headed up by a consultant (a doctor with a special interest in sleep). He may be supported by a number of more junior doctors, nurses and 'sleep technicians' who are trained to use specialist diagnostic equipment.

At the initial appointment the doctor is likely to go through your sleep diary and may order further tests to get to the cause of your insomnia. You may be invited in overnight for a polysomnography (sleep study). During this test you will have sensors known as electrodes placed on your body and head, and will have a 'bedroom' to sleep in overnight. Once you have dropped off to sleep, the electrodes pick up all sorts of different functions in your body. These could include:

- Brain activity.
- Eye movements.
- Jaw movements.
- Leg movements.
- Chest and stomach movement during breathing.
- Airflow.
- The amount of oxygen absorbed by your lungs.
- Heart activity.

Your sleep may also be filmed.

Quick action checklist

- Fill in a sleep diary over a week or more.
- Make an appointment with your doctor.

Summing Up

Getting to the bottom of your sleep problem can help you solve it. A sleep diary may shed new light on your problem and will help a doctor diagnose the cause. This is the first step to a better night's sleep.

Chapter Five

Your Bedroom

When you are having difficulties sleeping, it is important to spend some time thinking about your bedroom environment. All too often we forget about the importance of creating the right setting to fall asleep in. This chapter will explore how to make your bedroom a relaxing retreat from the outside world, helping you to consider environmental factors such as light and noise that may be preventing you from getting a good night's rest.

Creating a restful bedroom

Declutter

Take a good look at your bedroom and consider whether it is specifically designed to aid your rest. We all have our own tolerance with regards to how much mess we can accept but the first thing that you need to do is clear away any clutter that is in your room. Often, clutter can be a reminder of the jobs that you need to do in the day and it is not helpful to be reminded of these while you are trying to sleep. If you can't bear to throw things away, invest in some storage boxes and put them out of sight. Utilise space in your loft or garage and pack away any items that you don't use on a regular basis.

Ideally, your bedroom should only be used to sleep and have sex in. If you have part of it as a home office, it is worth considering whether you can move this equipment to another room in the house. Having a reminder about work in the bedroom does not help you to switch off and relax. A laundry basket that is constantly overflowing does not help to aid relaxation either and should be moved to another location like the bathroom or the landing.

'Take a good look at your bedroom and consider whether it is specifically designed to aid your rest.'

Watching television or playing computer games can actually stimulate your brain and stop you from sleeping. Do you really need a television in your bedroom? It may be better to take the television out and to watch it in another room.

Consider every item in your room and whether it really belongs in the bedroom. Think about how you treat the bedroom; do you treat it as a room for relaxation or as an extension of the living room? Do not take work to bed and avoid using your PC in the bedroom at all costs.

Set aside a day to work on clearing out the room. It's fine to have items displayed around the room as long as they are supposed to be there. Personalising with photographs or paintings that you love will help you to feel more connected with the room and aid relaxation.

'Take some time to consider the lighting in your room – you may wish to experiment with bulbs with a different wattage until you find one that you feel creates the right atmosphere.'

Creating the mood

Light and dark are very important for our sleep patterns – it is crucial that your body experiences both day and night time so that its natural circadian rhythm isn't disturbed. If light filters into the room, your body can think that it is time to wake up, even though you feel tired. As already mentioned, melatonin is the hormone that your body produces when it is dark – it causes you to feel tired. Therefore, a dark bedroom increases the amount of melatonin that you produce, making you feel drowsy.

Assess the curtains that you use – they should block out the light. If you have light coloured curtains, invest in some black out blinds to make sure that the early morning light does not creep in and cause you to wake up, particularly during the summer months. If your budget won't stretch to black out blinds, try draping a blanket over the curtains and see if you find this makes a difference to your sleep quality. Alternatively, you could try wearing an eye mask while you are sleeping.

If you haven't removed all electrical items from your bedroom, consider turning them all off at the mains each night. Equipment with LEDs can produce an invasive light when you are trying to get to sleep.

The lighting in your bedroom is extremely important in setting the mood for relaxation. A room that is too dark will feel oppressive and gloomy, while a room that is too bright may be difficult to relax in. Take some time to consider the lighting in your room – you may wish to experiment with bulbs with a different wattage until you find one that you feel creates the right atmosphere. Soft lighting and lamps are usually the best options for a bedroom. If your budget will stretch to it, you could consider dimmer switches so that you can control the amount of light used at different times of the day.

Colour

The colour of your bedroom can have a significant impact on the quality of your sleep. For example, bright colours tend to be less restful: fast food chains use them so that customers' visits are quick, enabling them to serve more diners.

Jess says: 'I decorated my bedroom red and white some years ago now and loved the finished result. But when I got into bed the first night, I was horrified. When the lights went out, the bedclothes and curtains seemed to be glowing in the dark! I found it incredibly distracting and just couldn't get to sleep. I tolerated it for a few months before deciding to re-decorate. I'd never use bright colours in a bedroom again after that experience!'

Choose the colour you use with relaxation in mind. You don't want to stimulate your senses. Soft pastel colours are very calming, particularly blues and greens.

'Research shows that smell can bring on a quick change of mood. Lavender can make a great scent to aid your relaxation.'

Scent

Research shows that smell can bring on a quick change of mood. Lavender can make a great scent to aid your relaxation. There are a number of lavender linen sprays on the market which are quick and easy to use – you just spray it directly onto your bedding. These sprays are inexpensive and may be worth trying out. Chapter 9 looks at aromatherapy and how essential oils can help promote restful sleep.

Comfort

Is your mattress comfortable? When was the last time you turned it over? It is important to rotate and turn most mattresses, ideally you should aim to turn yours at least once a month. This will help with wear and tear and will make sure that it is comfortable for longer. However, some modern mattresses do not require turning, so check the manufacturer's instructions.

You spend one third of your life in bed, so if you are sleeping on an old mattress it may be time to invest in a new one. A good quality mattress will support your spine and reduce the amount of tossing and turning you do during the night. Generally speaking, a mattress should be expected to last between seven and 10 years. However, the life span of your mattress will depend on its frequency of use, quality and wear and tear.

'You spend one third of your life in bed, so if you are sleeping on an old mattress it may be time to invest in a new one.'

If you answer yes to any of the following and your mattress is over seven years old, you may wish to consider buying a new one.

- Do you wake up with aches, stiffness and pains?
- Do you sleep better in hotels or at other people's homes than in your own bed?
- Has your mattress got signs of wear such as lumps or sags?
- Can you feel the bed springs or ridges in the bed when lying on it?
- When you get into bed can you hear any creaks from the mattress?

When choosing a new mattress, make sure that you test it properly. If you share a bed with someone, you need to lie on it at the same time to see how supportive it is. Try the mattress out using your usual sleeping position and have a go at rolling over. If the bed is too soft for you, this will be difficult! Mattress technology is changing all the time, so it is worth spending some time chatting to a salesperson to find out what is new on the market and which mattress will best meet your needs.

Pillows are also important in aiding a good night's sleep, so it's worth investing in some good quality pillows if you have a sleep problem. Finding the right pillow is very important and fortunately there are now many different types on the market. Everybody varies and finding the perfect pillow depends largely on your sleeping position. If you sleep on your back or stomach, you may prefer a thinner pillow to those who sleep on their side. Memory foam pillows mould to the shape of your neck and body, aligning posture and increasing blood circulation.

Another tip for helping you sleep is to check that your duvet is the correct tog for the time of year. If you are either becoming too hot or too cold during the night, you will wake up. All duvets are given a warmth rating measured in togs. The higher the tog, the warmer the duvet will be. If you are looking for a duvet for all seasons, you can now buy a combination duvet. This can be split into two separate duvets; a lightweight one suitable for the summer months and a medium weight one. The two can be fitted together to provide a high tog duvet for the winter months.

If you share your sleeping space and find that you have tussles with your partner for the duvet during the night, you could consider buying a duvet that is one size larger than your bed. Alternatively, copy tradition in certain continental European countries and have a single duvet each. This prevents arguments and allows each of you to choose the tog rating that suits you. This can work well if your partner is cold-blooded and your insomnia is worsened by overheating.

Noise

Some people are more sensitive to noise than others. If you think that noise may be disrupting your sleep, consider buying some earplugs. Alternatively, you could buy a white noise machine to drown out exterior noises. This is a devise that produces random sound patterns that block out external noises, and can be bought on the Internet. CDs that contain the whirring sound of white noise machines are also readily available, and you might even consider using a fan to help mask noises from both inside and outside the bedroom. Anything that blocks out noise is worth a try!

Do you have a clock in your bedroom? If this is ticking you could remove it and replace it with a digital clock. Listening to a clock ticking when you can't sleep can raise your stress levels, making it more difficult to fall back to sleep. Consider whether it is essential to have a clock in the bedroom on display. Sometimes clock watching can make you feel even more anxious if you can't get to sleep.

'Consider whether it is essential to have a clock in the bedroom on display. Sometimes clock watching can make you feel even more anxious if you can't get to sleep.'

Temperature

Make sure that the temperature in your bedroom is comfortable. Ideally, your bedroom should be slightly cooler; the temperature should be around 65°F or 18°C. Setting the room temperature helps to make sure that you aren't waking up in the night because you are too hot or too cold. You may wish to consider leaving the window slightly open so that air can circulate. If your bedroom is dry, you could buy a humidifier. Plants in the room help to produce oxygen and can bring moisture into dry environments.

Quick action checklist

- Have you decluttered your bedroom so that it is a restful retreat that promotes sleep?
- Does your mattress need replacing and are the pillows comfortable?
- Is the room at the right temperature and is fresh air circulating?
- Have you assessed the light and noise that enters your room?

Summing Up

Organising your bedroom to create a relaxing environment can feel a very positive thing to help combat your insomnia. Keeping the bedroom as a place for relaxation can help to set the scene for a good night's sleep.

Chapter Six

Tips to Promote Sleep

When you can't get to sleep (or stay asleep), you are willing to try anything to help drift off. This chapter will look at tips to get you off to sleep, many of them provided by fellow insomniacs. Follow the advice in this chapter to develop a routine that promotes a restful night's sleep.

Developing a good sleep routine

It is widely recognised that children need a good bedtime routine, but how much thought have you actually given to your own? It is essential to have an hour of relaxation prior to going to bed. We all tend to live hectic lifestyles and so it is sometimes necessary to plan the last hour of the day, ensuring you are going to bed feeling relaxed and ready to sleep.

Make a conscious effort to note what you do in the last hour before going to bed. If you are watching television, answering emails or trying to catch up on the household chores, you are most certainly not going to get into bed in a relaxed state. Take some time to work out a good routine that you can begin around an hour before you want to go to sleep.

You may wish to listen to music before bedtime. Choose the music that you listen to carefully – you are aiming to create a relaxed atmosphere, so hard rock and rousing brass music are best avoided! Instead, opt for classical music or easy listening. You should avoid anything that stimulates your mind such as television and computer games. If at all possible, dim the lights – bright light makes your body leap into action because it thinks that it's daytime!

Try to establish a regular bedtime and get up at the same time each day. As explained earlier, our sleep cycle is regulated by a circadian clock and it is important for the body to balance sleep time and wake time. By having a

'We all tend to live hectic lifestyles and so it is sometimes necessary to plan the last hour of the day, ensuring you are going to bed feeling relaxed and ready to sleep.'

regular wake time, you strengthen your body clock and this in turn can help with falling asleep at night. However, it can be difficult to stick to when you are tired, particularly on a weekend when you may have the opportunity to lie in.

Bath time

Some studies have suggested that having a bath at bedtime can help you to sleep better. It is important that you have the bath early on in your sleep routine so that your body temperature can regulate itself prior to going to bed. It is actually the change in body temperature that can lead to a better night's sleep. Your body temperature lowers after a bath and this can help you to drop off. There are a number of bath products on the market that claim to help relaxation and sleep – it may be worth exploring some of these to see if any of them do help.

Jean tells us: 'It may sound a silly suggestion, but if I can't sleep I get out of bed and wash my feet. When I get into bed, I fall asleep straightaway. My dad swore that this always helped him get to sleep if he was having trouble nodding off, so I tried it and it worked for me too!'

'You could make self massage a part of your sleep time routine, spending some time massaging your body and face until you feel calm and relaxed.'

Massage

Research has shown that massage can help promote sleep. Massage can be deeply relaxing and you don't have to be an expert to give a good one. Stroking and rubbing each other's skin is a natural and instinctive way of helping us to relax. If you have a partner, you could ask them to give you a foot massage following on from your bath. Alternatively, you could make self massage a part of your sleep time routine, spending some time massaging your body and face until you feel calm and relaxed. There are also a number of massaging devices available on the market that can help you to self massage; some systems also offer a soothing heat or gentle vibration.

Exercise

Exercise can help you feel tired and fall asleep, although you should plan when to take part in physical activity.

Exercising before bed can have the reverse effect and leave you feeling wide awake, so you should aim to exercise at least three hours before you plan to go to bed. Exercise in the late afternoon or early evening will raise your body temperature, allowing it to fall around bedtime which will help ease you to sleep. If you have any medical conditions, are overweight or have not been used to exercising, you should always talk to your doctor before starting an exercise regime.

Food and drink

Caffeine is a stimulant found in drinks such as coffee, tea, hot chocolate and cola. It can remain in the body for a number of hours and can even make some people feel alert for up to 12 hours after it is consumed. Therefore, it is best to avoid caffeine from mid afternoon.

Milky drinks are traditionally recommended to help sleep. Milk is full of calcium which can help soothe nerves and promote relaxation. However, be aware that many hot chocolate products may contain caffeine. Herbal teas are caffeine free and could be used as an alternative warm drink in the evenings.

When it comes to food, there are some that are thought to prevent restful sleep e.g. cheese. However, the British Cheese Board conducted a study in 2005 to determine the effect of cheese upon sleep and found that it had a positive effect. Likewise, some foods are thought to promote sleep. For example, eating a high carbohydrate meal two hours before you intend to go to sleep has been suggested as helpful for individuals who find getting to sleep difficult.

Your evening meal should not be too filling as overeating can cause sleep difficulties. Try keeping a food diary to see if there is a link between what you are eating during the day and your restlessness. Give your quality of sleep a score out of 10 each day with 10 being a fantastic night's sleep and one being terrible. Keep a diary for at least two weeks to accurately identify any patterns.

You may wish to consider whether you have a food allergy as this can cause poor sleeping. Food colourings, additives and preservatives should be avoided as these can aggravate insomnia. Links have also been found between high salt level intakes and insomnia. If you use salt in your cooking, you could make an effort to cut down as much as possible.

Food Diary	Breakfast	Lunch	Dinner	Sleep
Day 1				
Day 2				
Day 3				
Day 4				
Day 5				
Day 6				
Day 7				

Cigarettes and alcohol

While you may hear people saying they drink alcohol 'to relax', it can actually have the opposite effect.

- Drinking alcohol leads to the creation of adrenalin which stimulates your body and mind.
- If you drink alcohol in the evening, you are more likely to wake in the night to use the toilet, disturbing your sleep pattern further.
- Alcohol can often lead to you feeling thirsty which means you may wake during the night wanting a drink.

If you are concerned about the amount you are drinking, seek advice from a medical professional such as your doctor.

Research shows that smokers experience less of a deep sleep than non-smokers. Nicotine acts as a stimulant which can make falling asleep even more difficult. During the night smokers may also experience mild withdrawal from the nicotine, causing disturbed sleep. For help stopping smoking, contact Quit, the independent charity who aims to help smokers quit. Alternatively, the NHS now offers a wide range of support to encourage people to kick the habit. Details of how to contact both of these organisations can be found in the help list at the back of this book.

Heavy metal poisoning

Heavy metal poisoning is the build up of metals in the body to excessive levels. The most common heavy metals that you may be exposed to include aluminium, mercury and lead. Most people can excrete the toxins effectively, but some people are unable to, leading to an unhealthy build up.

Symptoms for heavy metal poisoning can be vague and it can be misdiagnosed as other conditions like autism or chronic fatigue syndrome. Chronic pain, fatigue and infections may be present, and sufferers may also suffer from neurological disorders, blurred vision, stomach complaints and mood swings. However, it is well documented that heavy metal poisoning can lead to sleep disorders, but it is rare in the UK. Follow the tips overleaf to reduce your exposure.

'Research shows that smokers experience less of a deep sleep than non-smokers. Nicotine acts as a stimulant which can make falling asleep difficult.'

- Do not use aluminium pots for cooking. Buy stainless steel or glass cookware instead.
- Don't use aluminium foil for cooking.
- Wash all fruit and vegetables before eating.
- Avoid using antacids that are aluminium based.
- Silver amalgam fillings in teeth should be avoided. If your old fillings need replacing, ask for composite or porcelain. Seek advice from your dentist.
- If you exercise near busy roads, plan out a new route so you can exercise away from the traffic.

Daytime naps

Do you take a nap in the daytime? If so, you could consider trying to substitute your usual nap with another sleep promoting activity such as going for a walk. If you do need a nap, consider setting an alarm. A 20 minute power nap can be helpful to recharge the batteries, but several hours in the day could seriously hinder your ability to sleep at night.

Worrying

If you lie in bed worrying about things that you should be doing, there is little wonder that you can't sleep. It can be helpful to write your worries down a couple of hours before you go to bed. Also try to plan out how you hope to alleviate your worries. If you become pre-occupied by thinking about your concerns when you are in bed, you can then remind yourself that they are all in hand and that you have identified ways forward.

Gail says: 'The best piece of advice I can offer to others with insomnia is to jot things down on a notepad that is kept next to the bed.'

When you can't get to sleep, you often lie in bed worrying about getting to sleep and about how tired you will feel in the morning. Remind yourself that although you are not asleep, your body and mind are becoming rested by lying in bed. Try to visualise a pleasant scene such as a tranquil beach. This should re-focus your mind and eliminate your worries.

Jane says: 'When I can't sleep, I begin to clock watch and worry about how dreadful I'm going to feel the next day. Now I try to fill my mind with pleasant thoughts. I think about a lovely holiday that we had in a cottage in the countryside. I imagine the feel of the summer breeze and the warm sun on my skin. I can feel the muscles in my body relaxing as I do this. Even if I don't fall asleep straight away, lying in bed with these pleasant thoughts is far better than worrying about the next day.'

Get up

If you can't get to sleep, get up. There is nothing worse than tossing and turning in bed, watching the clock. If you haven't nodded off after 30 minutes, get out of bed and do something non-stimulating such as listening to calm music. Return to bed when you feel tired.

'If you haven't nodded off after 30 minutes, get out of bed and do something non-stimulating such as listening to calm music.'

Quick action checklist

- Have you made sure that you have an hour to unwind before you go to bed?

- Does your sleep routine promote relaxation?

- Have you considered your diet and whether this is aggravating your difficulties?

- Are you worrying at night time? If so, have you started to jot your worries down and develop strategies to deal with them during the day?

Summing Up

Thinking about the time running up to bedtime can help you to develop a more relaxed routine. What you do in the daytime impacts on how well you sleep at night – from the food you eat to the activities that you carry out. Taking time out to consider these can have a positive impact on your sleep patterns.

Chapter Seven

Relaxation and Sleep

Many scientific studies have proven that learning to relax can be an effective treatment for insomnia. But when you are feeling stressed about sleep issues, feeling relaxed can be easier said than done. Studies have shown that individuals who actively practise relaxation fall to sleep more quickly, for longer periods and have a better quality of sleep. This chapter will provide you with simple techniques that you can use to help you to relax.

Am I stressed?

We all say that we are 'stressed' from time to time, but it may be helpful for you to consider whether you are actually suffering from stress. This could be making your insomnia worse, and if you aren't getting enough sleep this can make you feel more stressed – it can seem like a vicious cycle.

Tom says: 'You need to work out how to stop worrying about the insomnia. I found it was helpful to accept that I had insomnia. Getting stressed because you can't get to sleep is the worst thing that you can do.'

Consider when your insomnia first started. Did something stressful happen in your life around that time? Is the insomnia consistent throughout your life or is it worse when you are under stress?

Leah says: 'I've suffered bouts of insomnia throughout my life. I'd never really considered that they were stress related until I went to see a counsellor when my marriage broke down. As I started to tell her about my sleep problems, it emerged that every time I'd had these episodes something stressful had occurred in my life – some of the things I'd not actually acknowledged as being hugely stressful. I was in a minor car accident a few weeks ago and the

'We all say that we are "stressed" from time to time, but it may be helpful for you to consider whether you are actually suffering from stress.'

insomnia returned. I can now see why and am dealing with the stress that I feel about the accident by being more proactive, chasing up the insurers and sorting my car out. This has helped me to re-establish a good sleep pattern.'

Take a look at your life to see if you are able to determine the root cause of your stress. This could be your job, relationship, finances or other difficulties within the home.

Are you trying to do too much? The world that we live in is fast paced and sometimes we try to cram too much into 24 hours. Can you eliminate any of your commitments in order to reduce stress levels? Try making a 'to do' list. It can be incredibly satisfying ticking off the jobs you have completed.

If you can't get to sleep at night because you are worrying, try keeping a notepad by the bed. Writing down your worries can help clear your mind – you can deal with the problems the next day. Try to look at the situation you are worrying about from a different angle – see it as a challenge rather than as a threat. A change in viewpoint can help you take a more positive approach to stress.

In order to reduce your stress levels, you may need to do some creative thinking. Once you have identified what is causing you to feel stressed, you can take some positive action to reduce it. This may involve changing your attitude to certain situations or putting solutions in place to reduce your stress levels.

Sometimes you can be too close to a situation to see how to move it forward. You may wish to consider counselling so you have an opportunity to share your thoughts with a professional. Just talking about the stresses you face can be therapeutic. If you feel that your high stress levels are leading you to feel depressed or anxious, you should always consult your doctor for advice.

For more information, see *Stress - The Essential Guide* (Need2Know).

The importance of relaxation

Relaxation is vitally important – it helps to keep our stress levels down and improve our overall health and wellbeing. Studies have shown that relaxing on a regular basis has many benefits that include reducing the risk of heart attacks, improving the immune system, reducing the risk of mental health problems and, of course, aiding sleep.

Sometimes it can be difficult to find the time to relax and even if you do find the time, you may find that your mind wanders. It is important that you choose the right relaxation technique for you. Some people find a hot bath relaxing, while others enjoy listening to music or indulging in a hobby.

Now be honest, how much time do you allow yourself to relax? Relaxation need not be time consuming; just 10 minutes each day set aside to unwind can have a positive impact on your sleep difficulties. Make a commitment to factor in at least 10 minutes each day to forget the outside world and to enter a state of true relaxation. Relaxation should be enjoyable, so if you are not enjoying your chilling out time, it is perhaps time to rethink it. The ideas below should be helpful.

'Relaxation need not be time consuming; just 10 minutes each day set aside to unwind can have a positive impact on your sleep difficulties.'

Relaxing your mind

If you can relax your mind, your body will also unwind. Deep breathing can be very effective for lowering stress levels and relaxing the mind and body. When you breathe in deeply, you send calming signals to your brain. The brain then sends these signals to your body. There are a number of different breathing exercises that you can try, but the simplest to begin with is as follows.

- Sit in a comfortable position with one hand on your stomach and the other on your chest.
- Breath deeply through your nose, feeling your stomach pushing outwards. Your chest should remain still.
- Breathe out through your mouth while feeling your stomach go in, then use it to push all the air out.
- Take your time with each breath and repeat up to 10 times.

Some people find guided imagery a good way of relaxing. This is when you imagine yourself in a situation that you find relaxing. Just imagining yourself in a peaceful place can help to reduce your stress levels and leave you feeling calmer. Think about when you have felt relaxed – it might have been on a holiday or during a day trip to the seaside. Close your eyes and take a few deep breaths, imagining the scene. Add detail to your scene such as the scent of flowers or a gentle breeze in the air. Wander through the scene feeling more and more relaxed with each step that you take. Feel the calm and enjoy the relaxed state. When you are ready to return to the real world, count to three before opening your eyes.

This technique can be particularly useful for those with active minds because the mind is kept busy creating the imagery and it is easier to forget any worries.

Relaxing your body

When you become anxious, muscles in your body can tense up and interfere with you getting to sleep. Take 10 minutes to focus on your body in a quiet, peaceful place. Are you able to feel any tension in your muscles? Many people carry tension around their neck and shoulder areas. If you suspect that your body is feeling tense, you may benefit from using relaxation methods that are focused on your physical make up.

Progressive muscle relaxation (PMR) is a deep relaxation technique that is used to control stress and anxiety. It was described by Edmund Jacobson in the 1930s, who believed that mental calmness was a natural result of physical relaxation. The good news is that anybody can learn PMR and it only takes around 10 to 20 minutes each day to practise.

You can sit or lie down to practise PMR, just make sure that you are comfortable and that the environment is peaceful and free of distractions. Decide which muscle group you are going to start with – it is usually best to begin with the lower extremities and to end with the face or chest.

■ Begin by taking a deep breath and contracting a muscle group, e.g. your calf muscles for around 10 seconds.

■ As you breathe out, release the tension in the muscles.

- Allow yourself to relax for around 20 to 30 seconds before moving on to the next muscle group. As you breathe out, focus on the changes you feel when your body is relaxed.

- Some people like to imagine that they blow away their stressful feelings as they exhale.

- Work your way around all of the muscle groups in your body.

Many people suffering from insomnia have reported that using these techniques have been helpful in overcoming their sleep difficulties.

Nell says: 'I used to stay awake worrying about not being able to sleep. I went to yoga and learnt about progressive muscle relaxation. At the end of each class we would lay back and work on conscious muscle relaxation, working up from our toes and relaxing each muscle group in turn. This was enormously helpful and gave me something to focus on when trying to wind down at night. It really solved most of my sleep problems.'

Other relaxation techniques

Yoga

Exercise can help when you have difficulties sleeping. Yoga can be helpful for clearing the mind, ensuring that tensions from the body are released.

Rachael says: 'Yoga really helped me to relax. It worked so well for me – I was taught how to consciously relax myself and I have totally beaten insomnia.'

Yoga classes teach you poses but also may include instruction on breathing. If you are looking for a new hobby that may promote sleep, you may wish to consider trying a yoga class. Further information about how to find a class locally can be found in the help list.

'Yoga can be helpful for clearing the mind, ensuring that tensions from the body are released.'

Hypnotherapy

Hypnotherapy may be worth a try. A good hypnotherapist will show you how to use self hypnosis so that you can quickly relax at home. You may wish to visit a hypnotherapist at their practice or buy a hypnosis CD, allowing you to experience hypnosis from the comfort of your own home. More information about hypnotherapy is included in chapter 9.

Meditation

'Meditation is an approach that can be used by anyone to help them to cope with everyday life. It simply works by calming the mind.'

Some people find meditation a beneficial relaxation technique. Meditation simply works by calming the mind and is an approach that can be used by anyone to help them cope with everyday life. If stresses and tensions are preventing you from falling asleep, meditation can help you to achieve a relaxed mental state.

There are many different kids of meditation and many products on the market to teach you the art. If you feel that this is something that you would like to explore further, see the help list for more information.

Quick action checklist

- Have you identified any factors in your life that may be causing you stress? If so, have you taken positive action to address these?

- Do you make time for relaxation on a daily basis?

- Have you tried some of the techniques discussed in this chapter to promote relaxation?

Summing Up

We live in a fast paced world and it can be easy to forget the importance of relaxation and looking after ourselves. Don't feel guilty about taking time out for yourself – it is essential if you are going to stay healthy. Try to view relaxation as a necessary part of your new daily routine.

Chapter Eight

Remedies and Medication

If you are experiencing insomnia, you may want to find out whether there are drugs that can help you. However, there are pros and cons to taking medication to aid sleep. Sleeping tablets are highly addictive and can cause physical, psychological and other sleeping problems if you stop taking them suddenly. On the other hand, they do work and are useful in an emergency and for short term use.

This chapter helps you weigh up the factors for and against taking sleeping tablets. Over-the-counter drugs, herbal remedies and medication only available from the doctor are all considered.

Drugs and remedies you can buy

Herbs have been used to aid sleep for hundreds of years. However, there are few serious studies on the effects of different herbs on insomnia. Also, with any herbal remedy it is difficult to advise on a suitable dose as there is no standardisation of the way remedies are made.

You should always get medical advice before using herbs if you have a medical condition, take any medication, are pregnant or breastfeeding. Be careful about taking herbal remedies for insomnia if you have to drive or operate machinery the next day. Do not combine any of the herbs listed overleaf with other insomnia medications.

'Herbs have been used to aid sleep for hundreds of years.'

Natural remedies

Valerian

Valerian has undergone multiple studies and may help sleeplessness, although studies have been of variable quality and it is not clear how it works. Some people find it immediately effective, while others say it takes several weeks to start working. Valerian is the main ingredient in:

- Valerina Day-Time (also contains melissa/lemon balm).
- HRI Night (also contains passiflora, wild lettuce and hops).
- Kalms Sleep (also contains valerian, wild lettuce, passiflora, hops).

Chamomile

Chamomile is most often taken as tea. It can also be used in aromatherapy treatments with a few drops in massage oil or in the bath.

Lavender

Lavender is frequently used to aid sleep and relaxation; you can make or buy pillows filled with lavender, some people drink tea made with a few lavender heads and you can also try using a few drops of lavender essential oil for a relaxing bath before bed. It can even be used in aromatherapy treatments for insomnia.

See chapter 9 for more on complementary therapies.

Hops

A specific chemical contained in hops has a relaxing effect. A pillow filled with hops is a traditional remedy for sleeplessness, but the effectiveness of hops wears off after a few months as they lose their potency when exposed to light or air. Hops may be used alone in remedies, but they can also be combined with other herbs such as valerian.

'Chamomile is most often taken as tea. It can also be used in aromatherapy treatments with a few drops in massage oil or in the bath.'

Hops are the main ingredient in:

- Natrasleep (also contains valerian).

Passion flower

Passion flower (or Maypop) is reputed to be a mild sedative. It has been used in teas for insomnia in Native American traditional remedies. The leaves and roots in particular have chemical properties in common with MAOI (monoamine oxidase inhibitor) antidepressants.

Antihistamines

Some antihistamines are used as the basis of many of the over-the-counter sleep aids that you can buy from the pharmacy. They have a long lasting action so may leave you feeling drowsy the next day. As a result, you may need to avoid driving or operating machinery. The effectiveness of antihistamines decreases the longer you use them. You may not become physically addicted to this sort of drug but could feel that you can't get to sleep without it, known as psychological dependency. Antihistamines can also increase the effects of alcohol.

The antihistamine diphenhydramine hydrochloride is the active ingredient in:

- Boots' 'Sleepeaze'.
- Nytol.
- Dreemon.
- Medinex.
- Nightcalm.
- Panadol Night (together with paracetamol for pain).

The antihistamine promethazine hydrochloride is the active ingredient in:

- Phenergan Nightime.
- Sominex.

Antihistamines are not recommended for insomnia if you are pregnant or breastfeeding a baby. The drugs can cause problems if you have other medical conditions including:

- Asthma.

- Narrow angle glaucoma (raised pressure in the eye).

- Gastric or intestinal obstruction.

- Enlargement of the prostate.

- Bladder neck obstruction.

- Myasthenia gravis.

- Seizures.

'Sleeping tablets tend to be used by older people, with one in five people aged between 65 and 74 years using them.'

The newer antihistamines in many hayfever remedies do not cause sleepiness. Ask a pharmacist for advice.

Talk to your doctor or pharmacist if you have an existing medical condition or are taking any medication to make sure that a sleep remedy is compatible. Some medications and over-the-counter remedies can actually cause insomnia – get advice from a professional to make sure this is not the cause of your sleep problems.

Prescription medicines: drugs available only from your doctor

Have you thought about using sleeping tablets? They are not without drawbacks but can help you get out of a pattern of insomnia. Sleeping tablets tend to be used by older people, with one in five people aged between 65 and 74 years and almost a third of individuals 75 years or older using them.

Types of medication

Hypnotics are drugs that give you a feeling of calmness, relaxation and sleepiness. They slow your breathing and can reduce anxiety. Different types of hypnotics include barbiturates, benzodiazepines and non-benzodiazepine based drugs.

When medication is used

If you normally sleep well but are having problems due to jet lag, shift work or noise, your doctor may offer you few doses of a short acting hypnotic drug.

If you have short term insomnia due to stress or an illness, your doctor may offer you a short course of hypnotics. This means you take the drug for a week to three weeks to get some relief from the insomnia.

If you have chronic insomnia, drugs can provide temporary relief but you should not take them in the long term.

Depression can often be the cause of a disturbed night's sleep, especially leading to early waking. In this case your doctor should talk to you about treating the depression rather than the sleeplessness.

Depending on sleeping tablets

Any sleeping tablet or sedative can create psychological dependence. This means that you believe you cannot sleep without taking the tablet.

With hypnotics you can become used to them within three to 14 days which may make them less effective as time goes on. Alongside the risk of becoming dependent, this is another reason why doctors tend to prescribe only a week or fortnight's course of the drug.

Before taking sleeping tablets: questions to ask your doctor

If you are seriously considering using sleeping tablets, make sure you discuss the pros and cons with your doctor. Use the table overleaf and the points on page 81 to help you explore your options:

'If you are seriously considering using sleeping tablets, make sure you discuss the pros and cons with your doctor.'

Pros and cons of sleeping tablets	
Cons	**Pros**
Side effects such as headaches, drowsiness (!) memory problems and confusion.	Reliable way to go to sleep.
Impaired reaction time when driving or operating machinery – even if taken the previous night.	Can provide swift short term relief.
Psychological dependency.	
Physical dependency.	
May increase effect of alcohol.	
Withdrawal effects can include insomnia, anxiety and loss of appetite and can continue up to several months. You may have broken sleep and vivid dreams for some weeks.	
Can cause falls in older people.	

- Think about why you are having trouble sleeping.

- How much alcohol are you drinking? Although you may feel alcohol makes it easier for you to drop off, it can cause disturbed sleep.

- Have you taken simple steps like cutting out coffee, tea and chocolate before bed?

- Is there anything else that you can do, or be helped to do, before opting for sleeping tablets?

- Are you realistic about how much sleep you need?

Benzodiazepines

The most commonly used type of sleeping tablet is in the benzodiazepine family of drugs. Medical guidance suggests that this sort of drug should only be used for insomnia that is severe and disabling.

Benzodiazepines include drugs which have a long lasting effect – you may feel drowsy the next day. This includes:

- Nitrazepam.

Shorter acting benzodiazepines include drugs such as:

- Loprazolam.

- Lormetazepam.

- Temazepam.

These drugs leave less of a hangover the next day but are more likely to cause withdrawal problems.

If you have insomnia related to anxiety which is a problem during the day too, you might benefit from using a benzodiazepine with a longer term effect such as:

- Diazepam.

This sort of drug may not suit you if you have certain breathing problems, sleep apnoea (see chapter 1) or are pregnant or breastfeeding. They can also cause falls in older people. If you have an existing health condition, your doctor will take it into account when deciding on your medication.

Some people can feel more talkative and excited or even hostile and aggressive on these drugs. If you feel like this, talk to your doctor about altering the dose.

Be aware that this sort of drug can affect your ability to drive or do other skilled tasks. It can also increase the effects of alcohol.

Stopping benzodiazepines

When you are thinking about coming off benzodiazepine-type sleeping tablets, talk to your doctor first. Stopping tablets suddenly can make you feel confused or give you the shakes. Effects can occur within a few hours or take a few weeks to show, depending on whether your tablets are short or long acting.

Your doctor will suggest a programme where you gradually cut down the dose, so seek medical advice for your own individual situation.

Non-benzodiazepines

There are other drugs that act on the same receptors in your brain as benzodiazepines. These drugs are short acting, with the benefit of little or no hangover effect the next day. However, you should still be aware that this sort of drug can affect your ability to drive or do other skilled tasks. Again, the effects of alcohol can be increased by these drugs. Non-benzodiazepines include:

- Zopiclone (Zimovane).
- Zolpidem (Stilnoct).
- Zaleplon (Sonata).

These drugs are similar to benzodiazepines, prescribed for short periods only as they can be physically and psychologically addictive. They should not be stopped suddenly or without medical advice.

Deborah, 66, finds it easy to fall asleep but wakes in the early hours of the morning and is unable to get back to sleep. She says: 'This started when my husband was terminally ill. My doctor prescribed Zopiclone to help me get through such a difficult time. It gave me a solid night's sleep and didn't leave me drowsy the next day. If my husband needed help in the night, I felt able to wake and help him too. I've stopped taking it now, and the insomnia has returned.'

Antidepressants

Older antidepressants have a sedative effect and your doctor may occasionally suggest these for insomnia with depression. But these drugs have more side effects than their modern counterparts. They may alter your pattern of sleep and can be addictive.

Melatonin

Melatonin is a hormone which occurs naturally in your body. It is produced at night and in the dark and helps regulate when you sleep. It can be used to 'reset' your body clock and help with some sorts of insomnia. It has been available over the counter in the US for more than 15 years and has only recently become available in the UK on prescription. However, it's only for patients over 55 who suffer from insomnia that is not caused by any medical condition or by taking substances such as drugs or alcohol. It is taken an hour or two before bedtime.

Melatonin may have side effects for some people, e.g. irritability, restlessness and even insomnia, and is not advised for people with liver disease. A doctor can prescribe it for people who are under 55 'off licence' which means that it has not been proven safe for other groups. It is used in some children with special needs and sleep problems.

'Some medications and over-the-counter remedies can actually cause insomnia. Get advice from a professional to make sure this is not the cause of your sleep problems.'

Quick action checklist

- Have you tried other ways to deal with your insomnia as suggested in the previous chapters? Try these before using remedies or medication.

- Do you have other health conditions or take medication of any sort? If so, see your doctor for help.

- Talk to your pharmacist about remedies that are available over the counter. They will be able to help you weigh up the pros and cons.

Summing Up

Many people try herbal remedies for insomnia. A lavender pillow or cup of chamomile tea can be a simple way to relax at bedtime.

Prescription drugs can provide invaluable short term relief from insomnia but can cause problems if used in the long term, so seek medical advice. They are also highly addictive and can cause physical, psychological and sleep problems if you stop taking them suddenly.

Some medications and over-the-counter remedies can actually cause insomnia. Get advice from a professional to make sure this is not the cause of your sleep problems.

Chapter Nine

Complementary Therapies

Complementary therapies compliment conventional medical treatments. There is now a wide range of complementary therapies on offer and growing recognition that they can be beneficial to treat a range of disorders, including insomnia. Some complementary therapies are even available now on the NHS.

Many of the people that were spoken to during the research for this book have tried some form of complementary therapy in order to combat their insomnia. This chapter will give details about the different therapies on offer and how they claim to help with sleep difficulties.

Things to consider

Before you decide to visit a complementary therapist, there are a number of things you may need to consider.

- If you are taking medication or have a pre-existing health condition, you should consult your doctor.

- Many doctors now recognise that complementary therapies can have benefits. You should check to see if you are able to receive the therapy on the NHS.

- Make sure that you find a reliable practitioner and a professional body for the therapy that sets standards.

- If there is a cost implication for the therapy, find out first how much each session will be and how many sessions you are likely to need.

'There is now a wide range of complementary therapies on offer and growing recognition that they can be beneficial to treat a range of disorders, including insomnia.'

- When you choose a therapist, make sure you find somebody that you feel comfortable with.

- Don't be afraid to ask about the therapist's qualifications and whether they are a member of any professional bodies.

- You may also wish to ask about their experience of working with clients with sleep difficulties.

- Tell your practitioner if you are pregnant and be willing to disclose other medical conditions.

Practitioners of complementary therapies can register with a new regulatory body, the Complementary and Natural Healthcare Council which launched in 2009. The first professions to have standards in place for registration with the CNHC were massage therapy and nutritional therapy, followed by Alexander technique, aromatherapy, Bowen technique, cranial therapy, homeopathy, naturopathy, reflexology, reiki, shiatsu and yoga therapy.

Ask your practitioner if they have registered yet as this body aims to ensure quality in complementary therapies.

'Acupuncture can have a calming effect on clients and over time may help to correct imbalances causing insomnia.'

Types of complementary therapies you may consider

Acupuncture and acupressure

Acupuncture is part of traditional Chinese medicine and is based on the theory that energy flows along meridians in the body and can be stimulated by inserting fine needles into specific points. Depending on your condition, needles are inserted to varying depths from 4 to 25mm and left in place for varying lengths of time, from a few seconds up to 30 minutes or more. Disposable needles should be used.

Acupuncture can have a calming effect on clients and over time may help to correct imbalances causing insomnia. The first session can take up to 90 minutes and you will be asked about your medical history, emotional state, sleeping patterns and family history. The British Acupuncture Council is the

UK's main regulatory body for the therapy; their details can be found in the useful contacts section at the end of this book. The Council can help you to find out more about acupuncture and find a therapist in your area.

Acupressure is based on acupuncture; the fingers are used to create pressure on the key points of the body to stimulate healing. A specific pressure point on the inside of the wrist, just down from the little finger, is called H7. Acupressure cones gently massage this point and claim to help to promote natural sleep.

Boots produce Sleep Cones that work on this principle. An acupressure cone should be placed on each wrist and used for six nights, and then used alternative nights until sleep improves. The cones should not be used for more than two weeks when medical advice should then be sought.

Sharon has suffered from insomnia for over 10 years and has tried prescribed medicines as well as alternative therapies. She says: 'I use Sleep Cones and they have really helped. I also exercise on a regular basis and I find this is a fantastic way of overcoming insomnia.'

Aromatherapy

Aromatherapy is the use of essential oils to promote physical and emotional wellbeing. Each oil is extracted from a plant and is thought to have therapeutic properties.

Oils can be used in a number of different ways – by adding them to the bath water, massaging them into the skin or using them as a scent. If you choose to apply the oils directly to your skin, you must dilute them in oil first. You should seek out guidance from an aromatherapist about which oils are suitable to use, e.g. some oils should be avoided during pregnancy.

One of the easiest ways of using aromatherapy oils is in the bath: Roman chamomile and geranium oils promote relaxation, and lavender oil is calming and is claimed to be useful for insomnia and tension. Alternatively, you could put a couple of drops of oil onto a handkerchief and place it inside your pillow case.

Rachel says: 'I tried lavender sprays which were fantastic for my pregnancy insomnia but not so good now, after the birth.'

Aromatherapy oils can be bought in health stores, but you should always read the instructions carefully before using them. Alternatively, you could visit an aromatherapist, although you are advised to check that the therapist holds relevant qualifications. The Aromatherapy Council can provide you with further details about this – their details can be found in the help list.

Chiropractic

A chiropractor aims to improve mobility and relieve pain by manipulating joints and limbs. They take a holistic approach to their work and consider your symptoms by taking a full history of your lifestyle and personal circumstances. Importantly, it has been reported that spinal manipulation may improve symptoms of insomnia. This may have a relaxing effect on the nervous system which can help induce sleep.

You may also wish to consider seeing a chiropractor if you feel that your insomnia is due to discomfort during the night through back pain or another musculoskeletal disorder.

The General Chiropractic Council is a UK wide statutory body that regulates chiropractors. They can help you to find a local practitioner and answer questions that you may have about chiropractic. Contact details can be found in the help list.

Herbal medicine

Herbalism is the use of plants and herbal remedies. Herbalists prescribe herbs not only to alleviate the symptoms of insomnia, but also to correct the imbalances in the body that create the symptoms. A number of plants have sedative actions and are used to promote sleep. These include passion flower, hops, valerian, skullcap and chamomile.

Medical herbalist Dr Ann Walker says: 'Mild sleep problems can be helped by taking relaxing herbs at night before bedtime. Among the most popular are valerian and passiflora. However, nervine tonics like lemon balm and St John's Wort may also have a role if there is anxiety.

'If sleep problems are more severe, then it is probably due to adrenal dysfunction which can occur after long term stress. If adrenal function is depleted, this leads to a low secretion of cortisol. Sleep disturbance is very common in this condition. Adrenal function can be supported with the ginsengs or gotu cola. However, it is possibly better treated by a professional who has access to a wider range of adrenal supportive herbs.'

Herbal baths can aid relaxation and promote sleep – chamomile, linden flowers or lavender are ideal to be used in a bath. A handful of the herbs can be tied in a muslin bag and hung from the hot water tap. The fragrance will be released by the water and the properties of the herb will become activated. Once you get into the bath, your pores will open, allowing you to absorb the active parts of the herbs. You will also inhale the fragrance which will help to relax your body and mind.

The importance of carefully considering your bedtime drink has already been discussed. However, a cup of herbal tea can be calming half an hour before you go to bed. Lemon balm tea is also said to induce sleep. Pour boiling water over a couple of fresh leaves of the herb, steep for 10 minutes and drink slowly. Chamomile tea has mild sedative properties and can be bought in health stores.

If you are considering consulting a herbalist, it is advisable to find a practitioner that is registered with an organisation that is a member of the European Herbal and Traditional Medical Practitioners Association. See the help list for details.

'A number of plants have sedative actions and are used to promote sleep. These include passion flower, hops, valerian, skullcap and chamomile.'

Homeopathy

Homeopaths prescribe remedies for the whole person rather than just the sleep difficulty. If you go to visit a homeopath, they will spend a considerable amount of time focusing on you as an individual so that they can prescribe the correct remedy to treat your physical and emotional symptoms. There are a number of remedies that claim to help with sleep problems including coffea, ignatia and nux vomica.

Homeopathic remedies are diluted natural substances and are based on the theory of treating 'like with like'. The belief is that a diluted preparation of a substance given would in larger amounts produce similar symptoms to the condition being treated.

You can self-treat using homeopathic remedies which are available in health stores. You should select the remedy that most closely matches your symptoms. It may be worth investing in a book about the different remedies in order to find the correct one or you could ask for advice in store. If you prefer to see a qualified homeopath, you should contact the Society of Homeopaths who will be able to give you a list of registered practitioners in your area. Contact details can be found in the help list.

Hypnotherapy

'Indian head massage has been practised in India for generations to promote good health. The head, neck, shoulders and face are massaged to bring about a feeling of relaxation.'

Hypnotherapy is a method that is used to induce relaxation which can be helpful for sleep problems. A good hypnotherapist will teach you self hypnosis techniques that you can use at home. This will help you to reach a relaxed state. You can choose to visit a therapist or purchase a CD to listen to at home.

Lynn Wilshaw is a hypnotherapist and regularly works with clients who have sleep disorders. She says: 'I encourage people to look at their lifestyle in some detail. It is important to identify what is causing the sleep difficulty if we are to eliminate it. Teaching self-hypnosis is very helpful and can result in sleep disturbance being eliminated within a couple of weeks.' Contact details for Lynn can be found in help list at the back.

Joy purchased a CD in the hope that it would help with her insomnia: 'To get me to sleep I've tried everything without much success. But I found using a hypnotherapy CD very helpful. It was nice to just take the time to lie down and relax. My sleep pattern definitely improved and it was easier to fall asleep. I'd definitely recommend giving hypnotherapy a try.'

Massage

Massage can help to promote sleep. Aside from stimulating hormones, including endorphins, the feel good hormones, massage causes the blood and serotonin levels to rise. Serotonin plays a key role in sleep – it is needed to help our bodies produce melatonin. Therefore, increasing serotonin can have a positive impact on our sleep. Massage also soothes the central nervous system and can be used alongside aromatherapy oils.

There are a number of different types of massage that you may wish to try. Indian head massage has been practised in India for generations to promote good health. The head, neck, shoulders and face are massaged to bring about a feeling of relaxation. This can help to relieve tension, neck and shoulder stiffness, stress and insomnia. The massage is carried out fully clothed and usually lasts around 45 minutes.

Hot stone massage uses heated stones. The heat is said to help muscles to relax. The therapist may leave the stones on specific points of your body to improve energy flow. They may also hold the stones in their hands while massaging you.

Reflexology is based on the belief that there are reflexes in the hands and feet that relate to every organ in the body. During treatment the feet are massaged in specific ways to trigger reflex reactions within the body. Reflexology is a relaxing treatment that can help to reduce stress.

Bex Smith is a reflexologist from the Isle of Wight and runs her own business, 'Time for Reflexion'. Bex says: 'Reflexology is a holistic therapy. In other words, it treats the body and mind as a whole. It works on the basis that there are reflex points on both our hands and feet which when massaged can affect those areas of the body, either immediately or over time. It is closely linked to acupuncture but doesn't involve using needles. The whole process is incredibly relaxing, a therapist will ask you to sit in a special chair or lie on a couch and will massage each foot in turn to improve the circulation before following a set of specific reflexology massage techniques to treat each and every reflex. Once all the reflexes have been worked on, you will receive a lovely soothing massage, often with essential oils. Reflexology can be done on hands as well but is often less effective because hands tend to be tougher and less sensitive to the treatment.'

When it comes to using reflexology for sleep difficulties Bex advises, 'Try to find a mobile therapist to treat you in your own home. It would be preferable if you could have an appointment in the evening so that you can then go to bed feeling nicely relaxed.'

Contact details for Bex can be found in the help list.

Reiki

Reiki is a system of natural healing where the practitioner places their hands in a sequence of positions over the body drawing energy through the universe. The energy flows through their hands to the client's body and removes blockages that may be causing difficulties. Clothing does not have to be removed and Reiki is not intrusive. People experience Reiki in different ways – you may feel heat, a tingling sensation or a deep sense of relaxation.

Sam says: 'I'd had a terrible sleep pattern since I was diagnosed with chronic fatigue syndrome in my late teens. 10 years later I was still suffering and needed to take some positive action. I saw a lady advertising Reiki in your own home and decided it was worth a go. I've got to admit I was skeptical. Once she'd finished the first session, I felt incredibly relaxed and had my first good night's sleep for months. I continued to receive treatment and decided to become a practitioner myself. I'm now a Reiki Master and regularly use Reiki on myself if I'm finding it hard to sleep.'

Osteopathy

Osteopaths focus on the skeleton and joint functions, along with the muscles, soft tissues and internal organs. Osteopathy considers each person as an individual and uses touch to identify problem areas in the body. A full case history is taken on your first appointment and you can expect to be asked to carry out some simple movements so that the osteopath can assess your difficulties. They will use their highly developed sense of touch called 'palpation' to identify areas of weakness or strain in your body. Treatment usually begins by relaxing muscles and stiff joints, and manipulation may also be used. It is claimed that osteopathy can also provide insomniacs with benefits.

Cranial osteopathy is a gentle treatment where manipulative pressure is used to encourage the release of stress throughout the body, including the head. The General Osteopathic Council regulates practice in the UK and their contact details can be found in the help list.

Quick action checklist

■ Have you identified a complementary therapy that you may wish to try? If so, spend some time reading more about it so that you fully understand what will be involved.

■ Have you consulted your doctor before starting to use complementary therapy?

■ Is the therapist that you are using suitably qualified?

■ Do you feel comfortable with the therapist?

'Trying a new complementary therapy can make you feel as if you are doing something positive to address your sleep difficulties.'

Summing Up

Trying a new complementary therapy can make you feel as if you are doing something positive to address your sleep difficulties. Many of the therapies are relaxing and create a sense of wellbeing. Even if they don't solve your sleep problems, they will allow you to take some time out and enjoy relaxation.

Chapter Ten

Parenting a Teenager with Insomnia

If your teenager has sleep problems, they are not alone. Many teenagers suffer from sleep difficulties. The teenage years can be challenging enough with hormone changes, worries about self image and exam pressures. Sleep deprivation can make these issues seem far worse. This chapter examines what may be causing your child's sleep difficulties, strategies that may be helpful to address the problem and how you can support your teenager to develop a better sleep pattern.

Identifying the problem

Establishing that your child has a sleep difficulty can be challenging. Signs that there may be a disorder include:

- Inability to get to sleep.
- Waking several times in the night or early in the morning.
- Spending leisure time trying to catch up on their sleep.
- Sleepiness during the daytime.
- If you feel that your child's sleep pattern needs addressing, try to speak to them about it and make it clear that you want to offer them support.

Chloe says: 'As a teenager, I had an awful sleep pattern. I would be out socialising until the early hours of the morning and would be exhausted the following day. I spent the weekends asleep and my whole body clock was completely out of synch. When my mum approached me to talk about my sleep patterns, I was relieved to get some help. I didn't always like what she said but we negotiated so that we could find strategies to use that were acceptable to us both.'

Negotiation really is the key with teenagers. Unfortunately, it is likely that in order to improve their sleep they are going to have to make some changes to their lifestyle that they will not like. Take some time to talk with your teenager about their sleep habits and offer them support in addressing the issue.

Teenage lifestyles

As children get older, they can fall out of routine. They will usually be going to bed later than they were prior to their teenage years; many have busy social lives yet still have to be up early each morning to attend school, college or work. A hectic schedule can cause difficulty in falling asleep.

Teenagers' body clocks alter as they go through puberty. Melatonin is produced a few hours later than in childhood and therefore they will naturally want to go to sleep at a later time. We know that routine is helpful for addressing sleep disorders, therefore it would be beneficial if your teenager could begin to establish some structure to their day. 'Bedtime routine' sounds rather childish, so perhaps you could discuss it in other terms. 'Evening schedule' or 'night time activities' might sound more appropriate.

Teenagers may also begin to experiment with using stimulants which can interfere with sleep patterns. Alcohol, smoking and drugs can all have a direct impact on their sleep. If you are concerned that substance misuse may be an issue, it is important that you get support. Contact details for specialist organisations can be found in the help list. You should also seek the advice of a medical professional as soon as possible.

> 'As a direct result of tiredness, teenagers often begin to drink products containing caffeine during the day in order to try to stay alert. These can certainly aggravate sleep problems and their intake should be limited.'

As a direct result of tiredness, teenagers often begin to drink products containing caffeine during the day in order to try to stay alert. These could include coffee, cola or energy drinks. Such drinks can certainly aggravate sleep problems and their intake should be limited.

Teenagers need around 8.5 hours of sleep per night. Try keeping a sleep diary with your teen to see how many hours of sleep they are actually managing to get. You will find a copy of a sleep diary in chapter 4. It is also interesting to monitor your child's sleep pattern at weekends. Many teenagers try to catch up on their sleep which can make it even more difficult to readjust their sleep cycle, with their body finding it increasingly difficult to establish a pattern.

Stress

Being a teenager can be incredibly stressful. It is a period of transition, leaving childhood and entering adulthood. Teenagers can become anxious about many different issues such as:

- Examinations.
- Finding a job.
- Friendships.
- Experiencing their first relationship.
- Self image.
- Family issues.

Anxiety and depression can lead to insomnia and it is important that these underlying difficulties are identified and addressed. If you think that your child is suffering from anxiety related conditions, seek medical help and approach your doctor for support. Many schools and colleges offer counselling services where teenagers can share their anxieties – contact your child's educational setting to find out if they are able to offer support.

Tips for sleep

Here are some practical ideas that can be shared with your teenager to help them improve their sleep pattern.

- Encourage your teenager to go to bed at the same time each night; routine is vitally important to encourage good quality sleep.

'The teenage years can be challenging enough with hormone changes, worries about self image and exam pressures. Sleep deprivation can make these issues seem far worse.'

- Talk to your teenager about the importance of getting their body into a routine and setting an alarm so that they wake at the same time each day. Suggest that your teenager tries this but acknowledge that it can be difficult to stick to, especially at the weekend when a lie in is so tempting.

- Look at your teenager's bedtime routine and consider whether it is relaxing. Use tips in chapter 6 to establish how you can work together to make the period before bedtime more restful. Talk to your teenager about the importance of winding down time before they go to bed and discuss with them changes that could be made. Encourage them to come up with their own ideas about how their evening activities could be improved to promote better sleep patterns.

- Encourage your teenager to get out of bed if they haven't fallen asleep after half an hour. They should engage in a quiet activity and return to their bed when they feel tired. Devise a list of activities together as your teen may have different ideas about what helps them wind down. It is important that they associate their bed with going to sleep, therefore activities like watching television, playing video games and reading in bed should be discouraged.

- Suggest that you and your teenager assess their bedroom to see if it is providing them with a relaxing environment. Telephones, computer games and televisions can all provide unwelcome distractions when you are trying to get to sleep. Most teenagers will not want these to be removed but maybe a compromise could be made where it is agreed that these items will not be used between certain hours. Is the room dark enough? Investing in blackout blinds is an easy solution to blocking out light.

- Exercise can help with sleep disorders. If they don't already, suggest that your teenager exercises during the day. If your teenager finds it hard to unwind, look for classes with a relaxation element like yoga. Exercise should not be taken prior to bedtime.

- Consider what your teenager is drinking. Drinks containing caffeine should be avoided from lunch time onwards due to the stimulant effect they have.

- Is your teenager's schedule too demanding? Extra-curricular activities may need limiting. If they are doing too much in the daytime, they may be over-stimulated and have difficulties falling asleep.

'The good news is that most teenagers who have difficulties with sleep do grow out of it as their bodies adjust to a normal pattern after puberty.'

- Studying immediately before bedtime is not a good idea – it can stimulate the brain, making it more difficult to fall asleep. Work out a plan for homework and revision which allows for a break to wind down before bed.

- If these simple tips are not effective, it may be time to talk to your doctor. Complete a sleep diary with your teenager, as this will help with diagnosing the cause of the problem.

Quick action checklist

- Are you able to establish a cause for your child's sleep difficulties?

- Have you encouraged a bedtime routine?

- Have you considered their diet, activities and bedroom environment and the impact they may be having on sleep?

- Are you concerned that their sleep difficulties may be due to anxiety? If so, have you consulted a medical professional for support?

Summing Up

The teenage years are one of the most challenging periods of life. Chatting to your teenager about their sleep issues can be helpful in establishing any underlying cause. Supporting them to find solutions can help empower them to look at their own lifestyle and make the necessary adjustments to improve their sleep patterns. The good news is that most teenagers who have difficulties with sleep do grow out of it as their bodies adjust to a normal pattern after puberty.

Help List

Sleep organisations

NAPPS (Narcolepsy Action for Positive & Practical Solutions)

napps@cwcom.net
www.napps.cwc.net
NAPPS is a support group based in the UK providing support, advice and information for narcoleptics and other groups and individuals wishing to learn more about the condition.

Natural Sleep Foundation

81 Downs Road, Sutton, Surrey, SM2 5PR
Tel: 0208 642 3780
This group attempts to find the cause of sleeplessness and address the cause without the use of drugs. It can give information and support on daytime tiredness. They also offer a referral service if a medical cause is found.

Scottish Association for Sleep Apnoea (SASA)

secretary@scottishsleepapnoea.co.uk
www.scottishsleepapnoea.co.uk
SASA's aims are to increase public and professional understanding of sleep-related disorders and to reduce driving accidents and other problems associated with untreated sleep disorders.

The Sleep Apnoea Trust

12a Bakers Piece, Kingston Blount, Oxon, OX39 4SW
Tel: 0845 60 60 685
www.sleep-apnoea-trust.org
A charity of unpaid volunteers working to improve the lives of sleep apnoea

patients and their partners and families.

Sleep Solutions

Tel: 01432 355308
sleepsolutions@scope.org.uk
www.face2facenetwork.org.uk
Sleep Solutions offers support to families of children with a disability who also have sleep difficulties. They also offer training to parents and professionals.

Welsh Sleep Apnoea Society

Tel: 01633 774087
www.welshsas.org
This group aims to promote the understanding of breathing and sleep disorders. It does not provide medical advice.

Counselling

Cruse

PO Box 800, Richmond, Surrey, TW9 1RG
Tel: 0844 477 9400 (helpline)
helpline@cruse.org.uk
www.cruse.org.uk
A national charity that offers free confidential help to bereaved people. Cruse also offers support to young people.Young Person's helpline: 0808 808 1677
www.rd4u.org.uk.

Relate

Relate Central Office, Premier House, Cardina Court, Lakeside, Doncaster, DN4 5R4
Tel: 0300 100 1234
enquiries@relate.org.uk
www.relate.org.uk
Relate offers advice and relationship counselling through either face to face consultation, by telephone or through their website.

Health matters

Stop Smoking, Start Living

Tel: 0800 022 4332 (7am-11pm)
www.smokefree.nhs.uk
Detailed information about the free NHS support services to help smokers quit.

Talk to Frank

Tel: 0800 776600
frank@talktofrank.com
www.talktofrank.com
Advice and information for young people about drugs.

Quit

Tel: 0800 002200 (helpline)
stopsmoking@quit.org.uk
www.quit.org.uk
A charity that helps smokers quit and offers a confidential helpline.

Complementary therapy

The British Acupuncture Council

63 Jeddo Road, London, W12 9HQ
Tel: 020 8735 0400
info@acupuncture.org.uk
www.acupuncture.org.uk
The main regulatory body in the UK for acupuncture, providing information about registered practitioners.

CHIS-UK

info@chisuk.org.uk
www.chisuk.org.uk
A guide to complementary and alternative therapies.

Complementary and Natural Healthcare Council

83 Victoria Street, London, SW1H 0HW
Tel: 0203 178 2199
info@cnhc.org.uk
www.cnhc.org.uk
Register for massage therapy and nutritional therapy, followed by Alexander technique, aromatherapy, Bowen technique, cranial therapy, homeopathy, naturopathy, reflexology, reiki, shiatsu and yoga therapy.

European Herbal and Traditional Medicine Practitioners Association

Tel: 01684 291605
www.ehtpa.eu
The EHTPA represents professional associations of herbal/traditional medicine practitioners offering various western herbal medicine, chinese herbal medicine, Ayurveda and traditional Tibetan medicine.

General Chiropractic Council

44 Wicklow Street, London, WC1X 9HL
Tel: 020 7713 5155
enquiries@gcc-uk.org
www.gcc-uk.org
The body established to regulate chiropractors. Provides information to help you find a chiropractor.

General Osteopathic Council

176 Tower Bridge Road, London, SE1 3LU
Tel: 0207 357 6655
info@osteopathy.org.uk
www.osteopathy.org.uk
The body established to regulate osteopaths. Lists osteopaths who are registered to practice in the UK.

The National Institute of Medical Herbalists

Elm House, 54 Mary Arches Street, Exeter, EX4 3BA

Tel: 01392 426022
info@nimh.org.uk
www.nimh.org.uk
A leading professional body representing medical herbalists which can help you find a practitioner.

Society of Homeopaths

11 Brookfield, Duncan Close, Moulton Park, Northampton, NN3 6WL
Tel: 0845 450 6611
info@homeopathy-soh.org
www.homeopathy-soh.org
Provides information about homeopathy, including how to find a homeopath.

Meditation Class

info@meditationclass.co.uk
www.meditationclass.co.uk
Providers of meditation classes and workshops throughout the UK.

Yoga Village

www.yogauk.com
Site containing information about yoga including advice, resources and how to find an instructor.

Independent therapists

Lynn Wilshaw

Tel: 01302 742820
lynn@lynnwilshaw.co.uk
www.lynnwilshaw.co.uk
Hypnotherapist who specialises in sleep difficulties. CDs can be purchased to help with insomnia.

Sleep Success

info@sleepsuccess.co.uk

www.sleepsuccess.co.uk
Sleep service designing tailor made sleep programmes for both adults and children. It covers the whole of the UK.

Time for Reflexion

Tel: 01983 289982 (between 8.30am and 6pm only)
bex@time4reflexion.co.uk
www.time4reflexion.co.uk
Reflexology practice run by Bex Smith and based on the Isle of Wight.

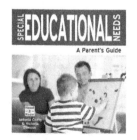

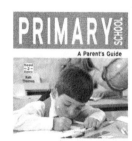

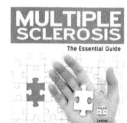

CPSIA information can be obtained at www.ICGtesting.com
Printed in the USA
LVOW02s1553080714

393412LV00003B/70/P